The Law School Admission Council (LSAC) is a nonprofit corporation whose members are more than 200 law schools in the United States, Canada, and Australia. Headquartered in Newtown, PA, USA, the Council was founded in 1947 to facilitate the law school admission process. The Council has grown to provide numerous products and services to law schools and to approximately 85,000 law school applicants each year.

All law schools approved by the American Bar Association (ABA) are LSAC members. Canadian law schools recognized by a provincial or territorial law society or government agency are also members. Accredited law schools outside of the United States and Canada are eligible for membership at the discretion of the LSAC Board of Trustees; Melbourne Law School, the University of Melbourne is the first LSAC-member law school outside of North America.

The services provided by LSAC are the Law School Admission Test (LSAT); the Credential Assembly Service, which includes letters of recommendation, electronic applications, and domestic and international transcript processing for JD degrees; the LLM Credential Assembly Service; the Candidate Referral Service (CRS); the Admission Communication & Exchange System (ACES, ACES^2); research and statistical reports; websites for law schools and prelaw advisors (*LSACnet.org*), law school applicants (*LSAC.org*), and undergraduates from minority groups (*DiscoverLaw.org*); testing and admission-related consultations with legal educators worldwide; and various publications, videos, and LSAT preparation tools. LSAC does not engage in assessing an applicant's chances for admission to any law school; all admission decisions are made by individual law schools.

LSAT, *The Official LSAT PrepTest*, *The Official LSAT SuperPrep*, *ItemWise*, and LSAC are registered marks of the Law School Admission Council, Inc. Law School Forums and LSAC Credential Assembly Service are service marks of the Law School Admission Council, Inc. *10 Actual, Official LSAT PrepTests*; *10 More Actual, Official LSAT PrepTests*; *The Next 10 Actual, Official LSAT PrepTests*; *The New Whole Law School Package*; *ABA-LSAC Official Guide to ABA-Approved Law Schools*; *Whole Test Prep Packages*; LSDAS; LLM Credential Assembly Service; ACES^2; ADMIT-LLM; *LSACnet*; Law School Admission Test; and Law School Admission Council are trademarks of the Law School Admission Council, Inc.

LSAC fees, policies, and procedures relating to, but not limited to, test registration, test administration, test score reporting, misconduct and irregularities, Credential Assembly Service (LSDAS), and other matters may change without notice at any time. Up-to-date LSAC policies and procedures are available at *www.LSAC.org*, or you may contact our candidate service representatives.

ISBN-13: 978-0-9760245-4-5
ISBN-10: 0-9760245-4-3

Print number
10 9 8 7 6 5 4

Table of Contents

The Law School Admission Test is a half-day standardized test required for admission to all ABA-approved law schools, most Canadian law schools, and many non-ABA-approved law schools. It consists of five 35-minute sections of multiple-choice questions. Four of the five sections contribute to the test taker's score. These sections include one reading comprehension section, one analytical reasoning section, and two logical reasoning sections. The unscored section, commonly referred to as the variable section, typically is used to pretest new test items and to preequate new test questions or to preequate new test forms. The placement of this section in the LSAT will vary. A 35-minute writing sample is administered at the end of the test. The writing sample is not scored by LSAC, but copies are sent to all law schools to which you apply. The score scale for the LSAT is 120 to 180.

The LSAT is designed to measure skills that are considered essential for success in law school: the reading and comprehension of complex texts with accuracy and insight; the organization and management of information and the ability to draw reasonable inferences from it; the ability to think critically; and the analysis and evaluation of the reasoning and arguments of others.

The LSAT provides a standard measure of acquired reading and verbal reasoning skills that law schools can use as one of several factors in assessing applicants.

For up-to-date information about LSAC's services, go to our website, *www.LSAC.org*.

Scoring

Your LSAT score is based on the number of questions you answer correctly (the raw score). There is no deduction for incorrect answers, and all questions count equally. In other words, there is no penalty for guessing.

■ Test Score Accuracy—Reliability and Standard Error of Measurement

Candidates perform at different levels on different occasions for reasons quite unrelated to the characteristics of a test itself. The accuracy of test scores is best described by the use of two related statistical terms: reliability and standard error of measurement.

Reliability is a measure of how consistently a test measures the skills being assessed. The higher the reliability coefficient for a test, the more certain we can be that test takers would get very similar scores if they took the test again.

LSAC reports an internal consistency measure of reliability for every test form. Reliability can vary from 0.00 to 1.00, and a test with no measurement error would have a reliability coefficient of 1.00 (never attained in practice). Reliability coefficients for past LSAT forms have ranged from .90 to .95, indicating a high degree of consistency for these tests. LSAC expects the reliability of the LSAT to continue to fall within the same range.

LSAC also reports the amount of measurement error associated with each test form, a concept known as the standard error of measurement (SEM). The SEM, which is usually about 2.6 points, indicates how close a test taker's observed score is likely to be to his or her true score. True scores are theoretical scores that would be obtained from perfectly reliable tests with no measurement error—scores never known in practice.

Score bands, or ranges of scores that contain a test taker's true score a certain percentage of the time, can be derived using the SEM. LSAT score bands are constructed by adding and subtracting the (rounded)

SEM to and from an actual LSAT score (e.g., the LSAT score, plus or minus 3 points). Scores near 120 or 180 have asymmetrical bands. Score bands constructed in this manner will contain an individual's true score approximately 68 percent of the time.

Measurement error also must be taken into account when comparing LSAT scores of two test takers. It is likely that small differences in scores are due to measurement error rather than to meaningful differences in ability. The standard error of score differences provides some guidance as to the importance of differences between two scores. The standard error of score differences is approximately 1.4 times larger than the standard error of measurement for the individual scores.

Thus, a test score should be regarded as a useful but approximate measure of a test taker's abilities as measured by the test, not as an exact determination of his or her abilities. LSAC encourages law schools to examine the range of scores within the interval that probably contains the test taker's true score (e.g., the test taker's score band) rather than solely interpret the reported score alone.

■ Adjustments for Variation in Test Difficulty

All test forms of the LSAT reported on the same score scale are designed to measure the same abilities, but one test form may be slightly easier or more difficult than another. The scores from different test forms are made comparable through a statistical procedure known as equating. As a result of equating, a given scaled score earned on different test forms reflects the same level of ability.

■ Research on the LSAT

Summaries of LSAT validity studies and other LSAT research can be found in member law school libraries.

■ To Inquire About Test Questions

If you find what you believe to be an error or ambiguity in a test question that affects your response to the question, contact LSAC by e-mail: *LSATTS@LSAC.org*, or write to Law School Admission Council, Test Development Group, Box 40, Newtown, PA 18940-0040.

How This PrepTest Differs From an Actual LSAT

This PrepTest is made up of the scored sections and the randomly assigned writing sample topics from the actual disclosed LSAT administered in December 2005. However, the reading comprehension section does not contain a comparative reading set (see page 4). Also, the PrepTest does not contain the extra, variable section that is used to pretest new test items of one of the three multiple-choice question types. The three multiple-choice question types may be in a different order in an actual LSAT than in this PrepTest. This is because the order of these question types is intentionally varied for each administration of the test.

The Question Types

The multiple-choice questions that make up most of the LSAT reflect a broad range of academic disciplines and are intended to give no advantage to candidates from a particular academic background.

The five sections of the test contain three different question types. The following material presents a general discussion of the nature of each question type and some strategies that can be used in answering them.

■ Analytical Reasoning Questions

Analytical reasoning items are designed to measure your ability to understand a structure of relationships and to draw logical conclusions about the structure. You are asked to make deductions from a set of statements, rules, or conditions that describe relationships among entities such as persons, places, things, or events. They simulate the kinds of detailed analyses of relationships that a law student must perform in solving legal problems. For example, a passage might describe four diplomats sitting around a table, following certain rules of protocol as to who can sit where. You must answer questions about the implications of the given information, for example, who is sitting between diplomats X and Y.

The passage used for each group of questions describes a common relationship such as the following:

- Assignment: Two parents, P and O, and their children, R and S, must go to the dentist on four consecutive days, designated 1, 2, 3, and 4;

- Ordering: X arrived before Y but after Z;

- Grouping: A manager is trying to form a project team from seven staff members—R, S, T, U, V, W, and X. Each staff member has a particular strength—writing, planning, or facilitating;

- Spatial: A certain country contains six cities and each city is connected to at least one other city by a system of roads, some of which are one-way.

Careful reading and analysis are necessary to determine the exact nature of the relationships involved. Some relationships are fixed (e.g., P and R always sit at the same table). Other relationships are variable (e.g., Q must be assigned to either table 1 or table 3). Some relationships that are not stated in the conditions are implied by and can be deduced from those that are stated. (e.g., If one condition about books on a shelf specifies that Book L is to the left of Book Y, and another specifies that Book P is to the left of Book L, then it can be deduced that Book P is to the left of Book Y.)

No formal training in logic is required to answer these questions correctly. Analytical reasoning questions are intended to be answered using knowledge, skills, and reasoning ability generally expected of college students and graduates.

Suggested Approach

Some people may prefer to answer first those questions about a passage that seem less difficult and then those that seem more difficult. In general, it is best not to start another passage before finishing one begun earlier, because much time can be lost in returning to a passage and reestablishing familiarity with its relationships. Do not assume that, because the conditions for a set of questions look long or complicated, the questions based on those conditions will necessarily be especially difficult.

Reading the passage. In reading the conditions, do not introduce unwarranted assumptions. For instance, in a set establishing relationships of height and weight among the members of a team, do not assume that a person who is taller than another person must weigh more than that person. All the information needed to answer each question is provided in the passage and the question itself.

The conditions are designed to be as clear as possible; do not interpret them as if they were intended to trick you. For example, if a question asks how many people could be eligible to serve on a committee, consider only those people named in the passage unless directed otherwise. When in doubt, read the conditions in their most obvious sense. Remember, however, that the language in the conditions is intended to be read for precise meaning. It is essential to pay particular attention to words that describe or limit relationships, such as "only," "exactly," "never," "always," "must be," "cannot be," and the like.

The result of this careful reading will be a clear picture of the structure of the relationships involved, including the kinds of relationships permitted, the participants in the relationships, and the range of actions or attributes allowed by the relationships for these participants.

Questions are independent. Each question should be considered separately from the other questions in its set; no information, except what is given in the original conditions, should be carried over from one question to another. In some cases a question will simply ask for conclusions to be drawn from the conditions as originally given. Some questions may, however, add information to the original conditions or temporarily suspend one of the original conditions for the purpose of that question only. For example, if Question 1 adds the information "if P is sitting at table 2 ...," this information should NOT be carried over to any other question in the group.

Highlighting the text; using diagrams. Many people find it useful to underline key points in the passage and in each question. In addition, it may prove very helpful to draw a diagram to assist you in finding the solution to the problem.

In preparing for the test, you may wish to experiment with different types of diagrams. For a scheduling problem, a calendar-like diagram may be helpful. For a spatial relationship problem, a simple map can be a useful device.

Even though some people find diagrams to be very helpful, other people seldom use them. And among those who do regularly use diagrams in solving these problems, there is by no means universal agreement on which kind of diagram is best for which problem or in which cases a diagram is most useful. Do not be concerned if a particular problem in the test seems to be best approached without the use of a diagram.

■ Logical Reasoning Questions

Logical reasoning questions evaluate your ability to understand, analyze, criticize, and complete a variety of arguments. The arguments are contained in short passages taken from a variety of sources, including letters to the editor, speeches, advertisements, newspaper articles and editorials, informal discussions and conversations, as well as articles in the humanities, the social sciences, and the natural sciences.

Each logical reasoning question requires you to read and comprehend a short passage, then answer one or two questions about it. The questions test a variety of abilities involved in reasoning logically and thinking critically. These include:

- recognizing the point or issue of an argument or dispute;

- detecting the assumptions involved in an argumentation or chain of reasoning;

- drawing reasonable conclusions from given evidence or premises;

- identifying and applying principles;

- identifying the method or structure of an argument or chain of reasoning;

- detecting reasoning errors and misinterpretations;

- determining how additional evidence or argumentation affects an argument or conclusion; and

- identifying explanations and recognizing resolutions of conflicting facts or arguments.

The questions do not presuppose knowledge of the terminology of formal logic. For example, you will not be expected to know the meaning of specialized terms such as "ad hominem" or "syllogism." On the other hand, you will be expected to understand and critique the reasoning contained in arguments. This requires that you possess, at a minimum, a college-level understanding of widely used concepts such as argument, premise, assumption, and conclusion.

Suggested Approach

Read each question carefully. Make sure that you understand the meaning of each part of the question. Make sure that you understand the meaning of each answer choice and the ways in which it may or may not relate to the question posed.

Do not pick a response simply because it is a true statement. Although true, it may not answer the question posed.

Answer each question on the basis of the information that is given, even if you do not agree with it. Work within the context provided by the passage. LSAT questions do not involve any tricks or hidden meanings.

■ Reading Comprehension Questions

The purpose of reading comprehension questions is to measure your ability to read, with understanding and insight, examples of lengthy and complex materials similar to those commonly encountered in law school work. The reading comprehension section of the LSAT contains four sets of reading questions, each consisting of a selection of reading material followed by five to eight questions. The reading selection in three of the four sets consists of a single reading passage of approximately 450 words in length. The other set contains two related shorter passages. Sets with two passages are a new variant of reading comprehension, called comparative reading, which were introduced into the reading comprehension section in June 2007. See "Comparative Reading" below for more information.

Reading selections for reading comprehension questions are drawn from subjects such as the humanities, the social sciences, the biological and physical sciences, and issues related to the law. Reading comprehension questions require you to read carefully and accurately, to determine the relationships among the various parts of the reading selection, and to draw reasonable inferences from the material in the selection. The questions may ask about the following characteristics of a passage or pair of passages:

- the main idea or primary purpose;

- the meaning or purpose of words or phrases used;

- information explicitly stated;

- information or ideas that can be inferred;

- the organization or structure;

- the application of information in a passage to a new context; and

- the author's attitude as it is revealed in the tone of a passage or the language used.

Suggested Approach

Since reading selections are drawn from many different disciplines and sources, you should not be discouraged if you encounter material with which you are not familiar. It is important to remember that questions are to be answered exclusively on the basis of the information provided in the selection. There is no particular knowledge that you are expected to bring to the test, and you should not make inferences based on any prior knowledge of a subject that you may have. You may, however, wish to defer working on a set of questions that seems particularly difficult or unfamiliar until after you have dealt with sets you find easier.

Strategies. In preparing for the test, you should experiment with different strategies and decide which work most effectively for you. These include:

- reading the selection very closely and then answering the questions;

- reading the questions first, reading the selection closely, and then returning to the questions; or

- skimming the selection and questions very quickly, then rereading the selection closely and answering the questions.

Remember that your strategy must be effective for you under timed conditions.

Reading the selection. Whatever strategy you choose, you should give the passage or pair of passages at least one careful reading before answering the questions. Try to distinguish main ideas from supporting ideas, and opinions or attitudes from factual, objective information. Note transitions from one idea to the next and examine the relationships among the different ideas or parts of a passage, or between the two passages in comparative reading sets. Consider how and why an author makes points and draws conclusions. Be sensitive to implications of what the passages say.

You may find it helpful to mark key parts of passages. For example, you might underline main ideas or important arguments, and you might circle transitional words—"although," "nevertheless," "correspondingly," and the like—that will help you map the structure of a passage. Moreover, you might note descriptive words that will help you identify an author's attitude toward a particular idea or person.

Answering the Questions

- Always read all the answer choices before selecting the best answer. The best answer choice is the one that most accurately and completely answers the question being posed.

- Respond to the specific question being asked. Do not pick an answer choice simply because it is a true statement. For example, picking a true statement might yield an incorrect answer to a question in which you are asked to identify an author's position on an issue, since here you are not being asked to evaluate the truth of the author's position but only to correctly identify what that position is.

- Answer the questions only on the basis of the information provided in the selection. Your own views, interpretations, or opinions, and those you have heard from others, may sometimes conflict with those expressed in a reading selection; however, you are expected to work within the context provided by the reading selection. You should not expect to agree with everything you encounter in reading comprehension passages.

■ Comparative Reading

As of the June 2007 administration, LSAC introduced a new variant of reading comprehension, called comparative reading, as one of the four sets in the LSAT reading comprehension section. In general, comparative reading questions are similar to traditional reading comprehension questions, except that comparative reading questions are based on two shorter passages instead of one longer passage. The two passages together are of roughly the same length as one reading comprehension passage, so the total amount of reading in the reading comprehension section remains essentially the same. A few of the questions that follow a comparative reading passage pair might concern only one of the two passages, but most will be about both passages and how they relate to each other.

Comparative reading questions reflect the nature of some important tasks in law school work, such as understanding arguments from multiple texts by applying skills of comparison, contrast, generalization, and synthesis to the texts. The purpose of comparative reading is to assess this important set of skills directly.

What Comparative Reading Looks Like

The two passages in a comparative reading set—labeled **"Passage A"** and **"Passage B"**—discuss the same topic or related topics. The topics fall into the same academic categories traditionally used in reading comprehension: humanities, natural sciences, social sciences, and issues related to the law. Like traditional reading comprehension passages, comparative reading passages are complex and generally involve argument. The two passages in a comparative reading pair are typically adapted from two different published sources written by two different authors. They are usually independent of each other, with neither author responding directly to the other.

As you read the pair of passages, it is helpful to try to determine what the central idea or main point of each passage is, and to determine how the passages relate to each other. The passages will relate to each other in various ways. In some cases, the authors of the passages will be in general agreement with each other, while in others their views will be directly opposed. Passage pairs may also exhibit more complex types of relationships: for example, one passage might articulate a set of principles, while the other passage applies those or similar principles to a particular situation.

Questions that are concerned with only one of the passages are essentially identical to traditional reading comprehension questions. Questions that address both passages test the same fundamental reading skills as traditional reading comprehension questions, but the skills are applied to two texts instead of one. You may be asked to identify a main purpose shared by both passages, a statement with which both authors would agree, or a similarity or dissimilarity in the structure of the arguments in the two passages. The following are additional examples of comparative reading questions:

- Which one of the following is the central topic of each passage?

- Both passages explicitly mention which one of the following?

- Which one of the following statements is most strongly supported by both passages?
- Which one of the following most accurately describes the attitude expressed by the author of passage B toward the overall argument in passage A?

- The relationship between passage A and passage B is most analogous to the relationship in which one of the following?

This is not a complete list of the sorts of questions you may be asked in a comparative reading set, but it illustrates the range of questions you may be asked.

For a sample comparative reading set, including explanations of the answers, go to *LSAC.org*, search for "comparative reading" in the search bar, and select "Preparing for the LSAT (PDF)," pages 9-14.

The Writing Sample

On the day of the test, you are required to write one sample essay. LSAC does not score the writing sample, but copies are sent to all law schools to which you apply. During the 2005–2006 testing year, you were randomly assigned one of two different kinds of writing prompt—decision or argument. In both cases the task was to deal with argument, either by constructing an argument for deciding in a certain way or by evaluating a given argument. You will have 35 minutes in which to plan and write an essay on the individual topic you receive. Current information can be found at *www.LSAC.org*.

The Decision Prompt

This kind of writing prompt presents a decision problem. You are asked to make a choice between two positions or courses of action. Both of the choices are defensible, and you are given criteria and facts on which to base your decision. There is no "right" or "wrong" position to take on the topic, so the quality of each test taker's response is a function not of which choice is made, but of how well or poorly the choice is supported and how well or poorly the other choice is criticized.

The Argument Prompt

This kind of writing prompt is designed to assess your ability to understand, analyze, and evaluate arguments and to clearly convey your evaluation in writing. The prompt consists of a brief passage in which the author makes a case for some course of action or interpretation of events by presenting claims backed by reasons and evidence. Your task is to discuss the cogency of the author's case by critically examining its line of reasoning and use of evidence.

Taking the PrepTest Under Simulated LSAT Conditions

One important way to prepare for the LSAT is to simulate the day of the test by taking a practice test under actual time constraints. Taking a practice test under timed conditions helps you to estimate the amount of time you can afford to spend on each question in a section and to determine the question types on which you may need additional practice.

Since the LSAT is a timed test, it is important to use your allotted time wisely. During the test, you may work only on the section designated by the test supervisor. You cannot devote extra time to a difficult section and make up that time on a section you find easier. In pacing yourself, and checking your answers, you should think of each section of the test as a separate minitest.

Be sure that you answer every question on the test. When you do not know the correct answer to a question, first eliminate the responses that you know are incorrect, then make your best guess among the remaining choices. Do not be afraid to guess as there is no penalty for incorrect answers.

When you take a practice test abide by all the requirements specified in the directions and keep strictly within the specified time limits. Work without a rest period. When you take an actual test you will have only a short break—usually 10-15 minutes—after SECTION III. When taken under conditions as much like actual testing conditions as possible, a practice test provides very useful preparation for taking the LSAT.

Official directions are included in this PrepTest so that you can approximate actual testing conditions as you practice.

To take the test:

- Set a timer for 35 minutes. Answer all the questions in SECTION I of this PrepTest. Stop working on that section when the 35 minutes have elapsed.

- Repeat, allowing yourself 35 minutes each for sections II, III, and IV.

- Set the timer for 35 minutes, then randomly pick one of the two writing sample topics and prepare your response to it.

- Refer to "Computing Your Score" for the PrepTest for instruction on evaluating your performance. An answer key is provided for that purpose.

The practice test that follows consists of four sections corresponding to the four scored sections of the December 2005 LSAT. Also reprinted are the two December 2005 unscored writing sample topics. Each test taker was randomly assigned to write one.

General Directions for the LSAT Answer Sheet

The actual testing time for this portion of the test will be 2 hours 55 minutes. There are five sections, each with a time limit of 35 minutes. The supervisor will tell you when to begin and end each section. If you finish a section before time is called, you may check your work on that section <u>only</u>; do not turn to any other section of the test book and do not work on any other section either in the test book or on the answer sheet.

There are several different types of questions on the test, and each question type has its own directions. <u>Be sure you understand the directions for each question type before attempting to answer any questions in that section.</u>

Not everyone will finish all the questions in the time allowed. Do not hurry, but work steadily and as quickly as you can without sacrificing accuracy. You are advised to use your time effectively. If a question seems too difficult, go on to the next one and return to the difficult question after completing the section. MARK THE BEST ANSWER YOU CAN FOR EVERY QUESTION. NO DEDUCTIONS WILL BE MADE FOR WRONG ANSWERS. YOUR SCORE WILL BE BASED ONLY ON THE NUMBER OF QUESTIONS YOU ANSWER CORRECTLY.

ALL YOUR ANSWERS MUST BE MARKED ON THE ANSWER SHEET. Answer spaces for each question are lettered to correspond with the letters of the potential answers to each question in the test book. After you have decided which of the answers is correct, blacken the corresponding space on the answer sheet. BE SURE THAT EACH MARK IS BLACK AND COMPLETELY FILLS THE ANSWER SPACE. Give only one answer to each question. If you change an answer, be sure that all previous marks are <u>erased completely</u>. Since the answer sheet is machine scored, incomplete erasures may be interpreted as intended answers. ANSWERS RECORDED IN THE TEST BOOK WILL NOT BE SCORED.

There may be more questions noted on this answer sheet than there are questions in a section. Do not be concerned but be certain that the section and number of the question you are answering matches the answer sheet section and question number. Additional answer spaces in any answer sheet section should be left blank. Begin your next section in the number one answer space for that section.

LSAC takes various steps to ensure that answer sheets are returned from test centers in a timely manner for processing. In the unlikely event that an answer sheet(s) is not received, LSAC will permit the examinee to either retest at no additional fee or to receive a refund of his or her LSAT fee. THESE REMEDIES ARE THE EXCLUSIVE REMEDIES AVAILABLE IN THE UNLIKELY EVENT THAT AN ANSWER SHEET IS NOT RECEIVED BY LSAC.

Score Cancellation

Complete this section only if you are absolutely certain you want to cancel your score. A CANCELLATION RE-QUEST CANNOT BE RESCINDED. IF YOU ARE AT ALL UNCERTAIN, YOU SHOULD <u>NOT</u> COMPLETE THIS SECTION.

To cancel your score from this administration, you **must**:

A. fill in both ovals here ..... ◯◯
    AND

B. read the following statement. Then sign your name and enter the date. **YOUR SIGNATURE ALONE IS NOT SUFFICIENT FOR SCORE CANCELLATION. BOTH OVALS ABOVE MUST BE FILLED IN FOR SCANNING EQUIPMENT TO RECOGNIZE YOUR REQUEST FOR SCORE CANCELLATION.**

I certify that I wish to cancel my test score from this administration. I understand that my request is irreversible and that my score will not be sent to me or to the law schools to which I apply.

_____
Sign your name in full

_____
Date

HOW DID YOU PREPARE FOR THE LSAT?
(Select all that apply.)

Responses to this item are voluntary and will be used for statistical research purposes only.

◯ By studying the sample questions in the *LSAT & LSDAS Information Book*.
◯ By taking the free sample LSAT in the *LSAT & LSDAS Information Book*.
◯ By working through official LSAT *PrepTests*, *ItemWise*, and/or other LSAC test prep products.
◯ By using LSAT prep books or software **not** published by LSAC.
◯ By attending a commercial test preparation or coaching course.
◯ By attending a test preparation or coaching course offered through an undergraduate institution.
◯ Self study.
◯ Other preparation.
◯ No preparation.

CERTIFYING STATEMENT
Please write (DO NOT PRINT) the following statement. Sign and date.

I certify that I am the examinee whose name appears on this answer sheet and that I am here to take the LSAT for the sole purpose of being considered for admission to law school. I further certify that I will neither assist nor receive assistance from any other candidate, and I agree not to copy or retain examination questions or to transmit them to or discuss them with any other person in any form.

_____
_____
_____
_____
_____
_____
_____
_____

SIGNATURE: _____   TODAY'S DATE: _____/_____/_____
                                                            MONTH DAY YEAR

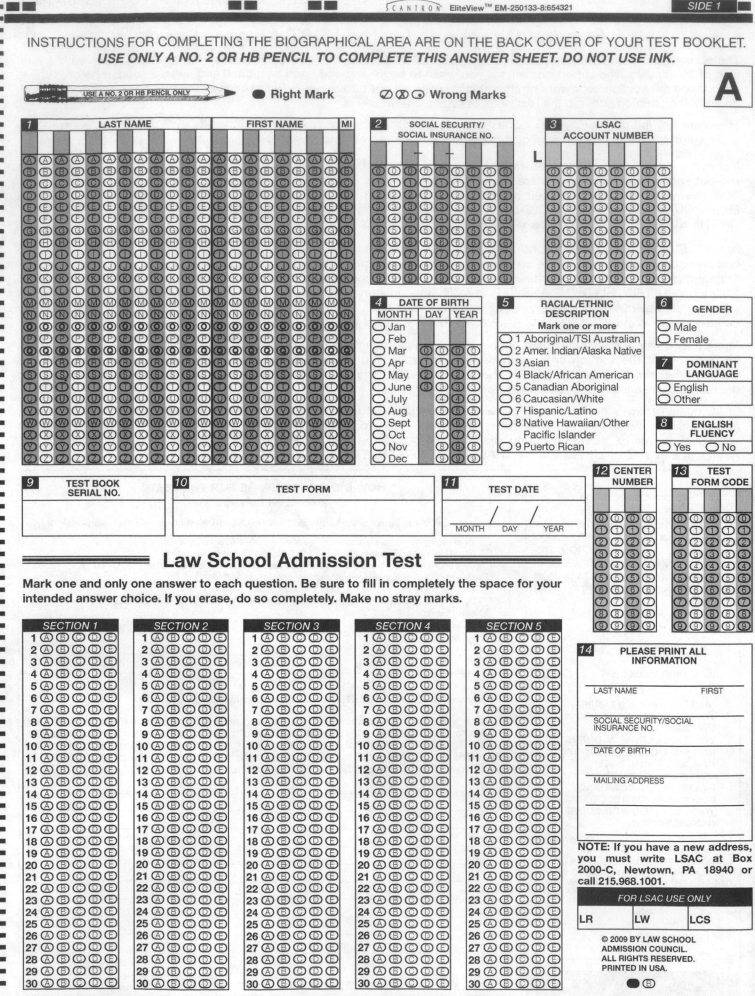

SECTION I

Time—35 minutes

26 Questions

<u>Directions:</u> The questions in this section are based on the reasoning contained in brief statements or passages. For some questions, more than one of the choices could conceivably answer the question. However, you are to choose the <u>best</u> answer; that is, the response that most accurately and completely answers the question. You should not make assumptions that are by commonsense standards implausible, superfluous, or incompatible with the passage. After you have chosen the best answer, blacken the corresponding space on your answer sheet.

1. The effort involved in lying produces measurable physiological reactions such as a speedup of the heartbeat. Since lying is accompanied by physiological reactions, lie-detector tests that can detect these reactions are a sure way of determining when someone is lying.

   Which one of the following statements, if true, most seriously weakens the argument?

   (A) Lie-detector tests can measure only some of the physiological reactions that occur when someone is lying.

   (B) People are often unaware that they are having physiological reactions of the sort measured by lie-detector tests.

   (C) Lying about past criminal behavior does not necessarily produce stronger physiological reactions than does lying about other things.

   (D) For people who are not lying, the tension of taking a lie-detector test can produce physiological reactions identical to the ones that accompany the act of lying.

   (E) When employers use lie-detector tests as part of their preemployment screening, some candidates tested are highly motivated to lie.

2. Publishing executive: Our company must sell at least 100,000 books to make a profit this year. However, it is unlikely that we will sell that many, since of the twelve titles we will sell, the one with the best sales prospects, a novel, is unlikely to sell as many as 100,000 copies.

   The publishing executive's argument is most vulnerable to criticism because it overlooks the possibility that

   (A) the publishing company will sell considerably fewer than 100,000 copies of the novel

   (B) the publishing company will not make a profit even if it sells more than 100,000 books

   (C) what is true of the overall profitability of a publishing company is not true of its profitability in a particular year

   (D) what is true of the sales prospects of the publishing company's individual titles is not true of the sales prospects of the group of titles as a whole

   (E) the publishing company will sell even fewer books if it does not advertise its books efficiently

3. A recent study proves that at least some people possess an independent "sixth sense" that allows them to detect whether someone is watching them. In the study, subjects were seated one at a time in the center of a room facing away from a large window. On average, subjects decided correctly 60 percent of the time whether or not they were being watched through the window.

   Which one of the following, if true, most supports the conclusion drawn from the study mentioned above?

   (A) Most of the time, subjects said they were being watched.

   (B) The person recording the experimental results was careful not to interact with the subjects after the experiment ended.

   (C) A similar result was found when the subjects were watched from another room on a video monitor.

   (D) The room in which the subjects were seated was not soundproof.

   (E) The subjects were mostly graduate students in psychology from a nearby university.

GO ON TO THE NEXT PAGE.

4. Philosopher: We should not disapprove of the unearthing of truths that we would rather not acknowledge or that, by their dissemination, might influence society in pernicious ways.

Which one of the following conforms most closely to the principle stated by the philosopher?

(A) A law enforcement officer should not act upon illegally obtained information, even though such action might, in some cases, result in a benefit to society.

(B) Scientific research should not be restricted even if it could lead to harmful applications, such as the manufacture of sophisticated weapons.

(C) A physician should never withhold the truth from a patient, except in cases where depression induced by bad news might significantly affect the patient's recuperation.

(D) Investigative journalists who employ illegal means of obtaining information should not be subjected to moral disapproval, if the revelation of that information does more good for society than does its suppression.

(E) A poem need not adhere too strictly to the truth. Art is exempt from such requirements—it matters only that the poem provoke a response in the reader.

5. Compact discs (CDs) offer an improvement in artistic freedom over vinyl records. As the record needle moves in toward a vinyl record's center, it must fight centrifugal force. Wide, shallow, or jagged grooves will cause the needle to jump; consequently, the song nearest the center—the last song on the side—cannot have especially loud, high-pitched, or low-pitched passages. The CD suffers no such limitations, leaving artists free to end recordings with any song.

Which one of the following most accurately expresses the main conclusion of the argument?

(A) CDs provide greater artistic latitude than do vinyl records.

(B) On vinyl records, the song farthest from the center can have loud, high-pitched, or low-pitched passages.

(C) As the record needle moves in toward the vinyl record's center, the centrifugal force on the needle becomes stronger.

(D) CDs represent a considerable technological advance over vinyl records.

(E) CDs can have louder passages, as well as both higher- and lower-pitched passages, than can vinyl records.

6. The public interest comprises many interests and the broadcast media must serve all of them. Perhaps most television viewers would prefer an action show to an opera. But a constant stream of action shows on all channels is not in the public interest. Thus, _____.

Which one of the following most logically completes the argument?

(A) broadcasters' obligations are not satisfied if they look only to popularity to decide their programming schedules

(B) television networks should broadcast more artistic and cultural shows and fewer action shows

(C) the public interest should be considered whenever television producers develop a new program

(D) the popularity of a television program is a poor indicator of its artistic quality

(E) broadcast media could be rightly accused of neglecting the public interest only if all channels carried mostly action shows

7. Enthusiasm for the use of calculators in the learning of mathematics is misplaced. Teachers rightly observe that in some cases calculators enable students to focus on general principles rather than the tedious, largely rote calculations that constitute the application of these principles. But principles are more likely to be remembered when knowledge of them is grounded in habits ingrained by painstaking applications of those principles. The very fact that calculators make calculation easier, therefore, makes it reasonable to restrict their use.

Which one of the following, if true, most strengthens the argument?

(A) Some students who know how to use calculators also thoroughly understand the mathematical principles that calculators obey.

(B) Slide rules, which are less technologically sophisticated analogues of calculators, were widely used in the learning of mathematics several decades ago.

(C) It is much more important that students retain the knowledge of general principles than that this knowledge be easily acquired.

(D) Habits that are acquired by laborious and sometimes tedious practice are not as valuable as those that are painlessly mastered.

(E) Teachers' enthusiasm for new educational aids is often not proportional to the pedagogical effectiveness of those devices.

GO ON TO THE NEXT PAGE.

8. Commentator: Most journalists describe their individual political orientations as liberal, and it is often concluded that there is therefore a liberal bias in current journalism. This is not the case, however, because newspapers, magazines, radio, and television are all in the business of selling news and advertising, and therefore face market pressures that tend to keep them impartial, since in order to maximize profits they must target the broadest customer base possible.

Which one of the following most accurately expresses the main conclusion drawn by the commentator's argument?

(A) The individual political orientations of journalists do not constitute acceptable evidence regarding media bias.

(B) Major media face significant market pressures.

(C) Current journalism does not have a liberal political bias.

(D) Major media must target the broadest customer base possible in order to maximize profits.

(E) It is often maintained that current journalism has a liberal bias.

9. Theories generated by scientific research were used to develop several products that, although useful, damage the environment severely. The scientists who conducted the research, however, should not be held responsible for that damage, since they merely generated the theories and could neither foresee nor restrict the kinds of products that might be designed using those theories.

Which one of the following principles, if established, justifies the conclusion above?

(A) Individuals who develop something that has desirable characteristics should not be held responsible for any undesirable characteristics that the thing has if improperly used.

(B) Individuals are justified in performing an activity that has both desirable and undesirable foreseeable consequences only if they alone bear its undesirable consequences.

(C) Individuals should receive credit for the foreseeable desirable consequences of the activities they perform only if those individuals are to be held responsible for any unforeseeable undesirable consequences those activities might have.

(D) Individuals who perform an activity should not be held responsible for any unforeseen undesirable consequences that arise from the use to which others put the results of that activity.

(E) Individuals should be held responsible for the foreseeable undesirable consequences of the activities that they perform and receive credit for the foreseeable desirable consequences of those activities.

10. The administration at a certain university has explained this year's tuition increase by citing increased spending on faculty salaries and on need-based aid to students. However, this year's budget indicated that faculty salaries constitute a small part of the university's expenditure, and the only significant increases in scholarship aid have gone to academic scholarships awarded regardless of need. The administration's explanation is not believable.

Which one of the following, if true, most strengthens the argument that the administration's explanation is not believable?

(A) With this year's budget, the university has increased its total spending on scholarship aid by 5 percent.

(B) With this year's budget, the university increased the allotment for faculty salaries by 5 percent while tuition was increased by 6 percent.

(C) Faculty salaries at the university have increased in line with the national average, and substantial cuts in government student-loan programs have caused financial difficulties for many students at the university.

(D) Of the substantial items in the budget, the greatest increase was in administrative costs, facilities maintenance costs, and costs associated with the provision of athletic facilities.

(E) Because enrollment projections at the university are very unreliable, it is difficult to accurately estimate the amount of money the university will collect from tuition fees ahead of time.

11. Students asked by a psychologist to tell a lie before discussion groups vastly overestimated how many people in the discussion groups could tell they were lying. Other research has found that when volleyball players perform unusually poorly on the court, teammates notice this far less often than the players expect. Finally, in one research experiment a student wearing a funny T-shirt entered a room full of people. Questioning revealed that only a small fraction of the people in the room noticed the shirt, contrary to the student's expectations.

Which one of the following is best illustrated by the statements above?

(A) People tend to be far less aware of their own appearance and behavior than are other people.

(B) People tend not to notice the appearance or behavior of others.

(C) We are actually less observant of the appearance and behavior of others than we think ourselves to be.

(D) People will notice the appearance or behavior of others only if it is specifically highlighted in some way.

(E) People tend to believe their appearance and behavior are noticed by others more often than is actually the case.

GO ON TO THE NEXT PAGE.

12. Extinction is inevitable for all biological species. In fact, the vast majority of all species that have ever lived are now extinct. Since all species die out eventually, there is no justification for trying to protect species that are presently endangered, even those that can be saved from extinction now.

The reasoning in the argument above is most closely paralleled by the argument that there is no reason to

(A) look for a book in the library because it is sometimes checked out
(B) spend money on preventive maintenance of a car because no car can last indefinitely
(C) reinforce bridges against earthquakes in earthquake-prone areas because earthquakes occur only very infrequently
(D) take a route that will avoid the normal traffic jams because traffic jams can occur along any route
(E) plant a flower garden in soil that is not beneficial to plants because the plants are likely to die in such soil

13. Psychology professor: Applied statistics should be taught only by the various social science departments. These departments can best teach their respective students which statistical methodologies are most useful for their discipline, and how best to interpret collected data and the results of experiments.

Mathematics professor: I disagree. My applied statistics course covers much of the same material taught in the applied statistics courses in social science departments. In fact, my course uses exactly the same textbook as those courses!

Which one of the following most accurately describes a questionable aspect of the reasoning in the mathematics professor's response to the psychology professor?

(A) The response gives no evidence for its presumption that students willing to take a course in one department would choose a similar course in another.
(B) The response gives no evidence for its presumption that social science students should have the same competence in statistics as mathematics students.
(C) The response does not effectively address a key reason given in support of the psychology professor's position.
(D) The response depends for its plausibility on a personal attack made against the psychology professor.
(E) The response takes for granted that unless the course textbook is the same the course content will not be the same.

14. Among a sample of diverse coins from an unfamiliar country, each face of any coin portrays one of four things: a judge's head, an explorer's head, a building, or a tree. By examining the coins, a collector determines that none of them have heads on both sides and that all coins in the sample with a judge's head on one side have a tree on the other.

If the statements above are true, which one of the following must be true of the coins in the sample?

(A) All those with an explorer's head on one side have a building on the other.
(B) All those with a tree on one side have a judge's head on the other.
(C) None of those with a tree on one side have an explorer's head on the other.
(D) None of those with a building on one side have a judge's head on the other.
(E) None of those with an explorer's head on one side have a building on the other.

15. There are two supposedly conflicting hypotheses as to what makes for great national leaders: one is that such leaders successfully shape public opinion, and the other is that they are adept at reacting to it. However, treating these hypotheses as mutually exclusive is evidently a mistake. All leaders who have had success getting their programs passed by their country's legislature have been adroit both in shaping and reacting to public opinion.

Which one of the following is an assumption on which the argument depends?

(A) Having success getting programs passed by the legislature is indicative of being a great national leader.
(B) It is impossible to successfully shape public opinion without in some way reacting to it.
(C) To lead, one must either successfully shape public opinion or be adept at reacting to it, or both.
(D) Having a good rapport with the members of the legislature allows a leader to shape public opinion.
(E) To be a great leader one must not be swayed by public opinion.

GO ON TO THE NEXT PAGE.

16. Most business ethics courses and textbooks confine themselves to considering specific cases and principles. For example, students are often given lists of ethical rules for in-class discussion and role-playing. This approach fails to provide a framework for understanding specific principles and should thus be changed to include abstract ethical theory.

Which one of the following, if valid, most helps to justify the reasoning above?

(A) A moralizing approach that fails to recognize the diversity of the ethical rules in use is unacceptable.

(B) Courses that concentrate mainly on role-playing are undesirable because students must adopt alien personae.

(C) People have no obligation to always behave ethically unless they are acquainted with abstract ethical theory.

(D) Abstract ethical theory is the most appropriate of any context for understanding specific principles.

(E) An ethics course should acquaint students with a wide range of specific principles and appropriate applications.

17. Some classes of animal are so successful that they spread into virtually every ecosystem, whereas others gradually recede until they inhabit only small niches in geographically isolated areas and thereby become threatened. Insects are definitely of the former sort and ants are the most successful of these, ranging from the Arctic Circle to Tierra del Fuego. Hence, no species of ant is a threatened species.

The argument is flawed because it takes for granted that

(A) the Arctic Circle and Tierra del Fuego do not constitute geographically isolated areas

(B) because ants do not inhabit only a small niche in a geographically isolated area, they are unlike most other insects

(C) the only way a class of animal can avoid being threatened is to spread into virtually every ecosystem

(D) what is true of the constituent elements of a whole is also true of the whole

(E) what is true of a whole is also true of its constituent elements

18. Advocate: You claim that it is wrong to own gasoline-powered cars because they pollute too much; you have an electric car, which pollutes far less. But the company that made your car also makes millions of gasoline-powered vehicles, so your patronage benefits a producer of products to which you object. Thus, if you are right about gasoline-powered cars, you should not have your electric car either.

Which one of the following principles, if valid, would most help to justify the advocate's reasoning?

(A) An action can be wrong even if it has fewer negative consequences than another action.

(B) One should purchase a product only if it pollutes less than any competing product.

(C) One should purchase every product whose use has no negative consequences.

(D) One should not support an organization that does anything one believes to be wrong.

(E) One should not purchase products from companies that make no environmentally sound products.

19. Analyst: A recent survey showed that although professors of biology who teach but do not pursue research made up one-twentieth of all science professors, they were appointed to fewer than one-twentieth of all the scientific administrative positions in universities. We can conclude from this survey that failing to pursue research tends to bias university administrators against appointing these professors to scientific administrative positions.

Which one of the following, if true, most seriously weakens the support for the analyst's conclusion?

(A) In universities there are fewer scientific administrative positions than there are nonscientific administrative positions.

(B) Biologists who do research fill a disproportionately low number of scientific administrative positions in universities.

(C) Biology professors get more than one-twentieth of all the science grant money available.

(D) Conducting biological research tends to take significantly more time than does teaching biology.

(E) Biologists who hold scientific administrative positions in the university tend to hold those positions for a shorter time than do other science professors.

GO ON TO THE NEXT PAGE.

20. Researcher: We have found that some cases of high
    blood pressure can be treated effectively with
    medicine. Since it is generally accepted that any
    illness caused by stress is treatable only by the
    reduction of stress, some cases of high blood
    pressure must not be caused by stress.

    Which one of the following is an assumption required
    by the researcher's argument?

    (A)   The correlation between stress and all cases of
          high blood pressure is merely coincidental.
    (B)   The reduction of stress in a person's life can at
          times lower that person's blood pressure.
    (C)   Reduced stress does not reduce a person's
          responsiveness to medicine used to treat high
          blood pressure.
    (D)   Some conditions that are treated effectively by
          medicines are not also treatable through the
          reduction of stress.
    (E)   Medicine used to treat high blood pressure does
          not itself reduce stress.

21. Catmull: Although historians consider themselves to be
    social scientists, different historians never arrive
    at the same conclusions about specific events of
    the past. Thus historians never determine what
    actually happened; like novelists, they merely
    create interesting fictional stories about the many
    different problems that people have faced.

    The reasoning in Catmull's argument is flawed because
    the argument

    (A)   draws a conclusion that simply restates a claim
          presented in support of that conclusion
    (B)   concludes, solely on the basis of the claim that
          different people have reached different
          conclusions about a topic, that none of these
          conclusions is true
    (C)   presumes, without providing justification, that
          unless historians' conclusions are objectively
          true, they have no value whatsoever
    (D)   bases its conclusion on premises that contradict
          each other
    (E)   mistakes a necessary condition for the objective
          truth of historians' conclusions for a sufficient
          condition for the objective truth of those
          conclusions

22. In a poll conducted by interviewing eligible voters in
    their homes just before the recent election, incumbent
    candidate Kenner was significantly ahead of candidate
    Muratori. Nonetheless, Muratori won the recent
    election.

    Which one of the following, if true, most helps to
    resolve the apparent discrepancy described by the
    statements above?

    (A)   The positions taken by Muratori and Kenner on
          many election issues were not very similar to
          each other.
    (B)   Kenner had held elected office for many years
          before the recent election.
    (C)   In the year leading up to the election, Kenner
          was implicated in a series of political scandals.
    (D)   Six months before the recent election, the voting
          age was lowered by three years.
    (E)   In the poll, supporters of Muratori were more
          likely than others to describe the election as
          important.

GO ON TO THE NEXT PAGE.

23. Statistical analysis is a common tool for explanation in the physical sciences. It can only be used, however, to explain events that can be replicated to the last detail. Since human mental events never precisely recur, statistical analysis cannot be employed to explain these events. Therefore, they cannot be explained by the physical sciences.

Which one of the following arguments is most similar in its flawed reasoning to the argument above?

(A) Computer modeling is used to try to explain the way in which wind resistance affects the movement of bicycles. To use computer modeling, the phenomenon being modeled must be predictable. But wind resistance is not predictable. Therefore, the way in which wind resistance affects the movement of bicycles cannot be explained by computer modeling.

(B) The only way to explain how music affects the emotional state of a person is to appeal to the psychology of emotion. The psychology of emotion can be applied only to cases involving human beings. But not all music is created by human beings; some music is computer generated. Therefore, the way in which music affects the emotional state of a person cannot be explained.

(C) The best way to explain why an object has a particular color is in terms of the interaction of light and matter. It is sometimes impossible to find out what kind of matter constitutes an object. Therefore, the color of such objects has nothing to do with the interaction of light and matter.

(D) To determine which explanation of the origin of the universe is correct, we would need to know about the first moments of the existence of the universe. Due to the immense time that has passed since the universe began, it is impossible to get such information. Therefore, none of the explanations of the origin of the universe is likely to be correct.

(E) A good way to explain historical events is to construct a coherent narrative about those events. In order to construct such a narrative, a great many details about the events must be known. Virtually no details can be known of certain very ancient historical events. Therefore, no historical explanation can be given for these events.

24. Journalist: Although a recent poll found that more than half of all eligible voters support the idea of a political party whose primary concern is education, only 26 percent would like to join it, and only 16 percent would be prepared to donate money to it. Furthermore, there is overwhelming historical evidence that only a party that has at least 30 percent of eligible voters prepared to support it by either joining it or donating money to it is viable in the long run. Therefore, it is unlikely that an education party is viable in the long run.

The reasoning in the journalist's argument is most vulnerable to criticism on the grounds that the argument fails to consider that

(A) some of those who said they were willing to donate money to an education party might not actually do so if such a party were formed

(B) an education party could possibly be viable with a smaller base than is customarily needed

(C) the 16 percent of eligible voters prepared to donate money to an education party might donate almost as much money as a party would ordinarily expect to get if 30 percent of eligible voters contributed

(D) a party needs the appropriate support of at least 30 percent of eligible voters in order to be viable and more than half of all eligible voters support the idea of an education party

(E) some of the eligible voters who would donate money to an education party might not be prepared to join such a party

GO ON TO THE NEXT PAGE.

25. Almost all microbe species live together in dense, interdependent communities, supporting the environment for each other, and regulating the population balances for their different species through a complex system of chemical signals. For this reason, it is currently impossible to cultivate any one such species in isolation. Thus, microbiologists lack complete knowledge of most microbe species.

Which one of the following, if assumed, enables the argument's conclusion to be properly drawn?

(A) It is currently impossible for microbiologists to reproduce the complex systems of chemical signals with which microbe communities regulate the population balances for their different species.

(B) If it is currently impossible to reproduce the environmental supports and chemical signals in dense, interdependent communities of microbe species, then it is also impossible to cultivate any microbe species from such a community in isolation.

(C) No microbiologist can have complete knowledge of any species of organism unless that microbiologist can cultivate that species in isolation.

(D) At least some microbiologists lack complete knowledge of any microbe species that live together in dense, interdependent communities.

(E) No microbe species that normally lives together with other microbe species in dense, interdependent communities can survive outside such a community.

26. Reza: Language requires the use of verbal signs for objects as well as for feelings. Many animals can vocally express hunger, but only humans can ask for an egg or an apple by naming it. And using verbal signs for objects requires the ability to distinguish these objects from other objects, which in turn requires conceptual thought.

If all of Reza's statements are true, then which one of the following must also be true?

(A) Conceptual thought is required for language.

(B) Conceptual thought requires the use of verbal signs for objects.

(C) It is not possible to think conceptually about feelings.

(D) All humans are capable of conceptual thought.

(E) The vocal expressions of animals other than humans do not require conceptual thought.

S T O P

IF YOU FINISH BEFORE TIME IS CALLED, YOU MAY CHECK YOUR WORK ON THIS SECTION ONLY.
DO NOT WORK ON ANY OTHER SECTION IN THE TEST.

SECTION II

Time—35 minutes

22 Questions

Directions: Each group of questions in this section is based on a set of conditions. In answering some of the questions, it may be useful to draw a rough diagram. Choose the response that most accurately and completely answers each question and blacken the corresponding space on your answer sheet.

Questions 1–6

Henri has exactly five electrical appliances in his dormitory room: a hairdryer, a microwave oven, a razor, a television, and a vacuum. As a consequence of fire department regulations, Henri can use these appliances only in accordance with the following conditions:

Henri cannot use both the hairdryer and the razor simultaneously.

Henri cannot use both the hairdryer and the television simultaneously.

When Henri uses the vacuum, he cannot at the same time use any of the following: the hairdryer, the razor, and the television.

1. Which one of the following is a pair of appliances Henri could be using simultaneously?

   (A)   the hairdryer and the razor
   (B)   the hairdryer and the television
   (C)   the razor and the television
   (D)   the razor and the vacuum
   (E)   the television and the vacuum

2. Assume that Henri is using exactly two appliances and is not using the microwave oven. Which one of the following is a list of all the appliances, other than the microwave oven, that Henri CANNOT be using?

   (A)   hairdryer
   (B)   razor
   (C)   vacuum
   (D)   hairdryer, razor
   (E)   hairdryer, vacuum

3. Which one of the following CANNOT be true?

   (A)   Henri uses the hairdryer while using the microwave oven.
   (B)   Henri uses the microwave oven while using the razor.
   (C)   Henri uses the microwave oven while using two other appliances.
   (D)   Henri uses the television while using two other appliances.
   (E)   Henri uses the vacuum while using two other appliances.

4. If Henri were to use exactly three appliances, then what is the total number of different groups of three appliances any one of which could be the group of appliances he is using?

   (A)   one
   (B)   two
   (C)   three
   (D)   four
   (E)   five

5. Which one of the following statements, if true, guarantees that Henri is using no more than one of the following: the hairdryer, the razor, the television?

   (A)   Henri is using the hairdryer.
   (B)   Henri is using the television.
   (C)   Henri is not using the hairdryer.
   (D)   Henri is not using the microwave oven.
   (E)   Henri is not using the vacuum.

6. Which one of the following must be true?

   (A)   Henri uses at most three appliances simultaneously.
   (B)   Henri uses at most four appliances simultaneously.
   (C)   Henri uses at most one other appliance while using the microwave oven.
   (D)   Henri uses at most one other appliance while using the razor.
   (E)   Henri uses at least two other appliances while using the hairdryer.

GO ON TO THE NEXT PAGE.

Questions 7–12

A farmer harvests eight separate fields—G, H, J, K, L, M, P, and T. Each field is harvested exactly once, and no two fields are harvested simultaneously. Once the harvesting of a field begins, no other fields are harvested until the harvesting of that field is complete. The farmer harvests the fields in an order consistent with the following conditions:

Both P and G are harvested at some time before K.
Both H and L are harvested at some time before J.
K is harvested at some time before M but after L.
T is harvested at some time before M.

7. Which one of the following could be true?

   (A)   J is the first field harvested.
   (B)   K is the second field harvested.
   (C)   M is the sixth field harvested.
   (D)   G is the seventh field harvested.
   (E)   T is the eighth field harvested.

8. If M is the seventh field harvested, then any one of the following could be the fifth field harvested EXCEPT:

   (A)   H
   (B)   J
   (C)   K
   (D)   L
   (E)   P

9. Which one of the following CANNOT be the field that is harvested fifth?

   (A)   G
   (B)   J
   (C)   M
   (D)   P
   (E)   T

10. If J is the third field harvested, then which one of the following must be true?

    (A)   L is the first field harvested.
    (B)   H is the second field harvested.
    (C)   T is the fourth field harvested.
    (D)   K is the seventh field harvested.
    (E)   M is the eighth field harvested.

11. If H is the sixth field harvested, then which one of the following must be true?

    (A)   G is harvested at some time before T.
    (B)   H is harvested at some time before K.
    (C)   J is harvested at some time before M.
    (D)   K is harvested at some time before J.
    (E)   T is harvested at some time before K.

12. If L is the fifth field harvested, then which one of the following could be true?

    (A)   J is harvested at some time before G.
    (B)   J is harvested at some time before T.
    (C)   K is harvested at some time before T.
    (D)   M is harvested at some time before H.
    (E)   M is harvested at some time before J.

GO ON TO THE NEXT PAGE.

Questions 13–17

In a repair facility there are exactly six technicians: Stacy, Urma, Wim, Xena, Yolanda, and Zane. Each technician repairs machines of at least one of the following three types—radios, televisions, and VCRs—and no other types. The following conditions apply:

Xena and exactly three other technicians repair radios.
Yolanda repairs both televisions and VCRs.
Stacy does not repair any type of machine that Yolanda repairs.
Zane repairs more types of machines than Yolanda repairs.
Wim does not repair any type of machine that Stacy repairs.
Urma repairs exactly two types of machines.

13. For exactly how many of the six technicians is it possible to determine exactly which of the three types of machines each repairs?

   (A)   one
   (B)   two
   (C)   three
   (D)   four
   (E)   five

14. Which one of the following must be true?

   (A)   Of the types of machines repaired by Stacy there is exactly one type that Urma also repairs.
   (B)   Of the types of machines repaired by Yolanda there is exactly one type that Xena also repairs.
   (C)   Of the types of machines repaired by Wim there is exactly one type that Xena also repairs.
   (D)   There is more than one type of machine that both Wim and Yolanda repair.
   (E)   There is more than one type of machine that both Urma and Wim repair.

15. Which one of the following must be false?

   (A)   Exactly one of the six technicians repairs exactly one type of machine.
   (B)   Exactly two of the six technicians repair exactly one type of machine each.
   (C)   Exactly three of the six technicians repair exactly one type of machine each.
   (D)   Exactly one of the six technicians repairs exactly two types of machines.
   (E)   Exactly three of the six technicians repair exactly two types of machines each.

16. Which one of the following pairs of technicians could repair all and only the same types of machines as each other?

   (A)   Stacy and Urma
   (B)   Urma and Yolanda
   (C)   Urma and Xena
   (D)   Wim and Xena
   (E)   Xena and Yolanda

17. Which one of the following must be true?

   (A)   There is exactly one type of machine that both Urma and Wim repair.
   (B)   There is exactly one type of machine that both Urma and Xena repair.
   (C)   There is exactly one type of machine that both Urma and Yolanda repair.
   (D)   There is exactly one type of machine that both Wim and Yolanda repair.
   (E)   There is exactly one type of machine that both Xena and Yolanda repair.

GO ON TO THE NEXT PAGE.

Questions 18–22

Three folk groups—Glenside, Hilltopper, Levon—and three rock groups—Peasant, Query, Tinhead—each perform on one of two stages, north or south. Each stage has three two-hour performances: north at 6, 8, and 10; south at 8, 10, and 12. Each group performs individually and exactly once, consistent with the following conditions:

Peasant performs at 6 or 12.
Glenside performs at some time before Hilltopper.
If any rock group performs at 10, no folk group does.
Levon and Tinhead perform on different stages.
Query performs immediately after a folk group, though not necessarily on the same stage.

18. Which one of the following could be a complete and accurate ordering of performances on the north stage, from first to last?

(A) Glenside, Levon, Query
(B) Glenside, Query, Hilltopper
(C) Hilltopper, Query, Peasant
(D) Peasant, Levon, Tinhead
(E) Peasant, Query, Levon

19. Which one of the following groups must perform earlier than 10?

(A) Glenside
(B) Hilltopper
(C) Levon
(D) Peasant
(E) Tinhead

20. Which one of the following groups could perform at 6?

(A) Glenside
(B) Hilltopper
(C) Levon
(D) Query
(E) Tinhead

21. If Query performs at 12, then which one of the following could be an accurate ordering of the performances on the north stage, from first to last?

(A) Glenside, Levon, Query
(B) Peasant, Hilltopper, Tinhead
(C) Peasant, Tinhead, Glenside
(D) Peasant, Tinhead, Hilltopper
(E) Peasant, Tinhead, Levon

22. If a rock group performs at 10, then which one of the following must be true?

(A) A folk group performs at 6.
(B) A folk group performs at 8.
(C) A folk group performs at 12.
(D) A rock group performs at 8.
(E) A rock group performs at 12.

S T O P

IF YOU FINISH BEFORE TIME IS CALLED, YOU MAY CHECK YOUR WORK ON THIS SECTION ONLY.
DO NOT WORK ON ANY OTHER SECTION IN THE TEST.

SECTION III
Time—35 minutes
27 Questions

Directions: Each passage in this section is followed by a group of questions to be answered on the basis of what is <u>stated</u> or <u>implied</u> in the passage. For some of the questions, more than one of the choices could conceivably answer the question. However, you are to choose the <u>best</u> answer; that is, the response that most accurately and completely answers the question, and blacken the corresponding space on your answer sheet.

One of the intriguing questions considered by anthropologists concerns the purpose our early ancestors had in first creating images of the world around them. Among these images are 25,000-year-
(5) old cave paintings made by the Aurignacians, a people who supplanted the Neanderthals in Europe and who produced the earliest known examples of representational art. Some anthropologists see these paintings as evidence that the Aurignacians had a
(10) more secure life than the Neanderthals. No one under constant threat of starvation, the reasoning goes, could afford time for luxuries such as art; moreover, the art is, in its latter stages at least, so astonishingly well-executed by almost any standard of excellence
(15) that it is highly unlikely it was produced by people who had not spent a great deal of time perfecting their skills. In other words, the high level of quality suggests that Aurignacian art was created by a distinct group of artists, who would likely have spent
(20) most of their time practicing and passing on their skills while being supported by other members of their community.

Curiously, however, the paintings were usually placed in areas accessible only with extreme effort
(25) and completely unilluminated by natural light. This makes it unlikely that these representational cave paintings arose simply out of a love of beauty or pride in artistry—had aesthetic enjoyment been the sole purpose of the paintings, they would presumably
(30) have been located where they could have been easily seen and appreciated.

Given that the Aurignacians were hunter-gatherers and had to cope with the practical problems of extracting a living from a difficult environment, many
(35) anthropologists hypothesize that the paintings were also intended to provide a means of ensuring a steady supply of food. Since it was common among pretechnological societies to believe that one can gain power over an animal by making an image of it,
(40) these anthropologists maintain that the Aurignacian paintings were meant to grant magical power over the Aurignacians' prey—typically large, dangerous animals such as mammoths and bison. The images were probably intended to make these animals
(45) vulnerable to the weapons of the hunters, an explanation supported by the fact that many of the pictures show animals with their hearts outlined in red, or with bright, arrow-shaped lines tracing paths to vital organs. Other paintings clearly show some
(50) animals as pregnant, perhaps in an effort to assure

plentiful hunting grounds. There is also evidence that ceremonies of some sort were performed before these images. Well-worn footprints of dancers can still be discerned in the clay floors of some caves, and
(55) pictures of what appear to be shamans, or religious leaders, garbed in fantastic costumes, are found among the painted animals.

1. Which one of the following most accurately describes the author's position regarding the claims attributed to anthropologists in the third paragraph?

   (A) implicit acceptance
   (B) hesitant agreement
   (C) noncommittal curiosity
   (D) detached skepticism
   (E) broad disagreement

2. The passage provides information that answers which one of the following questions?

   (A) For how long a period did the Neanderthals occupy Europe?
   (B) How long did it take for the Aurignacians to supplant the Neanderthals?
   (C) Did the Aurignacians make their homes in caves?
   (D) What are some of the animals represented in Aurignacian cave paintings?
   (E) What other prehistoric groups aside from the Aurignacians produced representational art?

GO ON TO THE NEXT PAGE.

3. The author would be most likely to agree with which one of the following statements?

   (A)   The cave paintings indicate that the Aurignacians lived a relatively secure life compared to most other hunter-gatherer cultures.

   (B)   Skill in art was essential to becoming an Aurignacian shaman.

   (C)   Prehistoric hunter-gatherers did not create any art solely for aesthetic purposes.

   (D)   All art created by the Aurignacians was intended to grant magical power over other beings.

   (E)   The Aurignacians sought to gain magical power over their prey by means of ceremonial acts in addition to painted images.

4. The author mentions the relative inaccessibility of the Aurignacian cave paintings primarily to

   (A)   stress the importance of the cave paintings to the lives of the artists who painted them by indicating the difficulties they had to overcome to do so

   (B)   lay the groundwork for a fuller explanation of the paintings' function

   (C)   suggest that only a select portion of the Aurignacian community was permitted to view the paintings

   (D)   help explain why the paintings are still well preserved

   (E)   support the argument that Aurignacian artists were a distinct and highly skilled group

5. The passage suggests that the author would be most likely to agree with which one of the following claims about the Aurignacians?

   (A)   They were technologically no more advanced than the Neanderthals they supplanted.

   (B)   They were the first humans known to have worn costumes for ceremonial purposes.

   (C)   They had established some highly specialized social roles.

   (D)   They occupied a less hostile environment than the Neanderthals did.

   (E)   They carved images of their intended prey on their weapons to increase the weapons' efficacy.

GO ON TO THE NEXT PAGE.

The poet Louise Glück has said that she feels comfortable writing within a tradition often characterized as belonging only to male poets. About her own experience reading poetry, Glück notes that
(5) her gender did not keep her from appreciating the poems of Shakespeare, Blake, Keats, and other male poets. Rather she believed this was the tradition of her language and that it was for this reason her poetic inheritance. She thus views the canon of poets in
(10) English as a literary family to which she clearly belongs. Whereas many contemporary women poets have rejected this tradition as historically exclusionary and rhetorically inadequate for women, Glück embraces it with respect and admiration.

(15) Glück's formative encounters with poetry also provided her with the theoretical underpinnings of her respect for this tradition; she notes that in her youth she could sense many of the great themes and subjects of poetry even before experiencing them in
(20) her own life. These subjects—loss, the passage of time, desire—are timeless, available to readers of any age, gender, or social background. Glück makes no distinction between these subjects as belonging to female or male poets alone, calling them "the great
(25) human subjects." If the aim of a poem is to explore the issue of human mortality, for example, then issues of gender distinction fade behind the presence of this universal reality.

Some of Glück's critics claim that this idea of the
(30) universal is suspect and that the idea that gender issues are transcended by addressing certain subjects may attribute to poetry an innocence that it does not have. They maintain that a female poet writing within a historically male-dominated tradition will on some
(35) level be unable to avoid accepting certain presuppositions, which, in the critics' view, are determined by a long-standing history of denigration and exclusion of female artists. Furthermore, they feel that this long-standing history cannot be confronted
(40) using tools—in Glück's case, poetic forms—forged by the traditions of this history. Instead critics insist that women poets should strive to create a uniquely female poetry by using new forms to develop a new voice.

(45) Glück, however, observes that this ambition, with its insistence on an essentially female perspective, is as limiting as her critics believe the historically male-dominated tradition to be. She holds that to the extent that there are some gender differences that have been
(50) shaped by history, they will emerge in the differing ways that women and men write about the world— indeed, these differences will be revealed with more authority in the absence of conscious intention. She points out that the universal subjects of literature do
(55) not make literature itself timeless and unchanging. Literature, she maintains, is inescapably historical, and every work, both in what it includes and in what it omits, inevitably speaks of its social and historical context.

6. Which one of the following most accurately expresses the main point of the passage?

(A) In response to her critics, Glück argues that the attempt to develop a uniquely female voice is as restrictive as they believe the male tradition in poetry to be.

(B) Although critics have taken Glück to task for writing poetry that is generic in subject rather than specifically aimed at addressing women's concerns, she believes that poetry must instead concern itself with certain universal themes.

(C) In spite of critics who attempt to limit art to expressing the unique perspectives of the artist's gender, Glück believes that art in fact represents a perspective on its subject matter that is equally male and female.

(D) In opposition to some critics, Glück writes on universal themes rather than striving for a uniquely female voice, believing that whatever gender differences are present will emerge unconsciously in any case.

(E) Aside from the power and accomplishment of her writing, Glück has yet to offer a completely satisfying response to the critics' demand that her work reflect the conflict between male and female perspectives on poetic subject matter.

7. Based on the passage, with which one of the following statements regarding the poetic tradition in English would Glück be most likely to agree?

(A) This tradition is somewhat diminished for its lack of recognized female poets.

(B) This tradition transcends its social and historical context.

(C) The male-dominated aspect of this tradition can be overcome only by developing a uniquely female voice in poetry.

(D) The view of this tradition as an inheritance is necessary for a poet to be successful.

(E) This tradition, though male dominated, addresses universal subjects.

GO ON TO THE NEXT PAGE.

8. As it is used in the passage, "inheritance" (line 9) refers most specifically to

   (A) the burden that a historically male-dominated poetic canon places on a contemporary woman poet
   (B) the set of poetic forms and techniques considered acceptable within a linguistic culture
   (C) the poetry written in a particular language, whose achievement serves as a model for other poets writing in that language
   (D) the presumption that contemporary poets can write only on subjects already explored by the poets in that language who are considered to be the most celebrated
   (E) the imposition on a poet, based on the poetry of preceding generations in that language, of a particular writing style

9. Based on the description in the passage, a poem that reveals gender differences in the absence of any specific intention by the poet to do so is most like

   (A) a bird's flight that exposes unseen air currents
   (B) a ship's prow that indicates how strong a wave it is designed to withstand
   (C) a building's facade that superficially embellishes an ordinary structure
   (D) a railroad track, without which travel by train is impossible
   (E) a novel that deliberately conceals the motives of its main character

10. According to the passage, Glück believes that art reveals gender differences with more authority when which one of the following is true?

   (A) The artist refuses to accept certain presuppositions about gender.
   (B) The artist uses the tools of that art's tradition.
   (C) The artist does not consciously intend to reveal such differences.
   (D) The artist comments on gender issues through the use of other subject matter.
   (E) The artist embraces that art's tradition with respect.

11. Which one of the following statements about Glück is made in the passage?

   (A) She objects to the use of traditional poetic forms to confront the history of the poetic tradition.
   (B) She recognizes that the idea of the universal in poetry is questionable.
   (C) She claims to accept only male poets as her literary family.
   (D) She claims to write from a gender-neutral perspective.
   (E) She claims to have sensed the great themes and subjects of poetry while in her youth.

12. Based on the passage, which one of the following most accurately characterizes the author's attitude toward Glück's view of poetry?

   (A) respectful dismissal
   (B) grudging acceptance
   (C) detached indifference
   (D) tacit endorsement
   (E) enthusiastic acclaim

GO ON TO THE NEXT PAGE.

Although the rights of native peoples of Canada have yet to be comprehensively defined in Canadian law, most native Canadians assert that their rights

(5) include the right not only to govern themselves and their land, but also to exercise ownership rights over movable cultural property—artifacts ranging from domestic implements to ceremonial costumes. Assignment of such rights to native communities has been difficult to achieve, but while traditional

(10) Canadian statute and common law has placed ownership of movable property with current custodians such as museums, recent litigation by native Canadians has called such ownership into question.

(15) Canadian courts usually base decisions about ownership on a concept of private property, under which all forms of property are capable of being owned by individuals or by groups functioning legally as individuals. This system is based on a

(20) philosophy that encourages the right of owners to use their property as they see fit without outside interference. But litigation by native Canadians challenges courts to recognize a concept of property ownership that clashes with the private property

(25) concept. Although some tribes now recognize the notion of private property in their legal systems, they have traditionally employed a concept of collective ownership—and in all cases in which native Canadians have made legal claim to movable

(30) property they have done so by invoking this latter concept, which is based on the philosophy that each member should have an equal say regarding the use of the community's resources. Under this collective ideology, access to and use of resources is determined

(35) by the collective interests of the community. Furthermore, collective ownership casts an individual in the role of guardian or caretaker of property rather than as a titleholder; while every tribe member is an owner of the property, individual members cannot sell

(40) this right, nor does it pass to their heirs when they die. Nevertheless, their children will enjoy the same rights, not as heirs but as communal owners.

Because the concept of collective property assigns ownership to individuals simply because they are

(45) members of the community, native Canadians rarely possess the legal documents that the concept of private property requires to demonstrate ownership. Museums, which are likely to possess bills of sale or proof of prior possession to substantiate their claims

(50) of ownership, are thus likely to be recognized as legally entitled to the property they hold, even when such property originated with native Canadian communities. But as their awareness of the inappropriateness of applying the private property

(55) concept to all cultural groups grows, Canadian courts will gradually recognize that native Canadians, while they cannot demonstrate ownership as prescribed by the notion of private property, can clearly claim ownership as prescribed by the notion of collective

(60) property, and that their claims to movable cultural property should be honored.

13. Which one of the following most accurately expresses the main idea of the passage?

(A) Litigation by native Canadians to regain control of their movable cultural property illustrates how the concept of private ownership has become increasingly obsolete and demonstrates that this concept should be replaced by the more modern concept of collective ownership.

(B) Litigation by native Canadians to regain control of their movable cultural property is likely to succeed more frequently as courts begin to acknowledge that the concept of collective ownership is more appropriate than the concept of private ownership in such cases.

(C) The conflict between the concepts of collective and private ownership that has led to litigation by native Canadians to regain control of their movable cultural property is in reality a debate over whether individuals should act as titleholders or merely as caretakers with respect to their property.

(D) The conflict between the concepts of collective and private ownership that has led to litigation by native Canadians to regain control of their movable cultural property cannot be resolved until the rights of native Canadians have been comprehensively defined in Canadian law.

(E) The conflict between the concepts of collective and private ownership that has led to litigation by native Canadians to regain control of their movable cultural property illustrates the need to expand the concept of private property to include cases of joint ownership by a collection of individuals.

14. According to the concept of private property as presented in the passage, which one of the following most completely describes the meaning of the term "property owner"?

(A) one who possesses a bill of sale to substantiate his or her claims to property ownership

(B) one who possesses proof of prior possession to substantiate his or her claims to property ownership

(C) one who is allowed to make use of his or her property in whatever manner he or she wishes

(D) one who is allowed to transfer ownership rights to his or her children as heirs

(E) one who is allowed to exercise property rights because of his or her membership in a community

GO ON TO THE NEXT PAGE.

15. The author's attitude toward the possibility of courts increasingly assigning ownership rights to native communities is best described as which one of the following?

    (A) certain that it will never be realized and concerned that it should
    (B) concerned that it will never be realized but hopeful that it will
    (C) uncertain whether it will be realized but hopeful that it will
    (D) uncertain whether it will be realized but confident that it should
    (E) convinced that it will be realized and pleased that it will

16. The primary function of the first paragraph of the passage is to

    (A) identify some of the specific types of property at issue in litigation by native Canadians to regain control of their movable cultural property from museums
    (B) describe the role of the concept of property ownership in litigation by native Canadians to regain control of their movable cultural property from museums
    (C) summarize the difficulties that have been experienced in attempting to develop a comprehensive definition of the rights of native Canadians under the law
    (D) provide the context within which litigation by native Canadians to regain control of their movable cultural property is occurring
    (E) discuss the difficulty of deciding legal cases that rest on a clash between two cultures' differing definitions of a legal concept

17. Given the information in the passage, Canadian courts hearing a dispute over movable cultural property between a museum and a group of native Canadians will be increasingly unlikely to treat which one of the following as a compelling reason for deciding the case in the museum's favor?

    (A) The museum is able to produce evidence that the property did not originate in the native community.
    (B) The museum cannot produce written documentation of its claims to ownership of the property.
    (C) The group of native Canadians produces evidence that the property originated in their community.
    (D) The group of native Canadians cannot produce written documentation of their claims to ownership of the property.
    (E) The group of native Canadians do not belong to a tribe that employs a legal system that has adopted the concept of private property.

18. The passage suggests that the concepts of collective and private ownership differ in each of the following ways EXCEPT:

    (A) The collective concept allows groups of individuals to own property; the private concept does not.
    (B) The collective concept requires consideration of community interests; the private concept does not.
    (C) The collective concept assigns ownership on the basis of membership in a community; the private concept does not.
    (D) The private concept allows owners to function as titleholders to their property; the collective concept does not.
    (E) The private concept permits individuals to sell property; the collective concept does not.

19. The passage most supports which one of the following statements about the tribal legal systems mentioned in the second paragraph of the passage?

    (A) All tribes whose legal system employs the concept of collective property have engaged in litigation over control of movable cultural property.
    (B) Only tribes that have engaged in litigation over control of movable property have a legal system that employs the concept of collective property.
    (C) All tribes that have engaged in litigation over control of movable cultural property have a legal system that employs the concept of collective property.
    (D) All tribes whose legal system recognizes the concept of private property can expect to succeed in litigation over control of movable cultural property.
    (E) Only those tribes whose legal system recognizes the concept of private property can expect to succeed in litigation over control of movable cultural property.

GO ON TO THE NEXT PAGE.

The first thing any embryo must do before it can develop into an organism is establish early polarity—that is, it must set up a way to distinguish its top from its bottom and its back from its front. The
(5) mechanisms that establish the earliest spatial configurations in an embryo are far less similar across life forms than those relied on for later development, as in the formation of limbs or a nervous system: for example, the signals that the developing fruit fly uses
(10) to know its front end from its back end turn out to be radically different from those that the nematode, a type of worm, relies on, and both appear to be quite different from the polarity signals in the development of humans and other mammals.

(15) In the fruit fly, polarity is established by signals inscribed in the yolklike cytoplasm of the egg before fertilization, so that when the sperm contributes its genetic material, everything is already set to go. Given all the positional information that must be
(20) distributed throughout the cell, it takes a fruit fly a week to make an egg, but once that well-appointed egg is fertilized, it is transformed from a single cell into a crawling larva in a day. By contrast, in the embryonic development of certain nematodes, the
(25) point where the sperm enters the egg appears to provide crucial positional information. Once that information is present, little bundles of proteins called p-granules, initially distributed uniformly throughout the cytoplasm, begin to congregate at one end of the
(30) yolk; when the fertilized egg divides, one of the resulting cells gets all the p-granules. The presence or absence of these granules in cells appears to help determine whether their subsequent divisions will lead to the formation of the worm's front or back
(35) half. A similar sperm-driven mechanism is also thought to establish body orientation in some comparatively simple vertebrates such as frogs, though apparently not in more complex vertebrates such as mammals. Research indicates that in human
(40) and other mammalian embryos, polarity develops much later, as many stages of cell division occur with no apparent asymmetries among cells. Yet how polarity is established in mammals is currently a tempting mystery to researchers.

(45) Once an embryo establishes polarity, it relies on sets of essential genes that are remarkably similar among all life forms for elaboration of its parts. There is an astonishing conservation of mechanism in this process: the genes that help make eyes in flies
(50) are similar to the genes that make eyes in mice or humans. So a seeming paradox arises: when embryos of different species are at the one- or few-cell stage and still appear almost identical, the mechanisms of development they use are vastly different; yet when
(55) they start growing brains or extremities and become identifiable as distinct species, the developmental mechanisms they use are remarkably similar.

20. Which one of the following most accurately expresses the main point of the passage?

(A) Species differ more in the mechanisms that determine the spatial orientation in an embryo than they do in their overall genetic makeup.

(B) Embryos determine their front from their back and top from bottom by different methods, depending on whether the organism is simple or more complex.

(C) While very similar genes help determine the later embryonic development of all organisms, the genetic mechanisms by which embryos establish early polarity vary dramatically from one organism to the next.

(D) The mechanisms by which embryos establish early polarity differ depending on whether the signals by which polarity is achieved are inscribed in the cytoplasm of the egg or the p-granules of the sperm.

(E) Despite their apparent dissimilarity from species to species, the means by which organisms establish polarity rely on essentially the same genetic mechanisms.

21. The passage suggests that the author would be most likely to agree with which one of the following statements?

(A) The simpler the organism, the greater the speed at which it develops from fertilized egg to embryo.

(B) Scientists have determined how polarity is established in most simple vertebrates.

(C) Scientists will try to determine how polarity is established in humans.

(D) Very few observations of embryonic development after polarity is established are generalizable to more than a single species.

(E) Simpler organisms take longer to establish polarity than do more complex organisms.

GO ON TO THE NEXT PAGE.

22. The passage provides information to suggest that which one of the following relationships exists between the development of humans and the development of fruit flies?

(A) Since humans and fruit flies use similar genetic material in their development, analogies from fruit fly behavior can be useful in explaining human behavior.

(B) For the elaboration of parts, human development relies on genetic material quite different in nature, though not in quantity, from that of a fruit fly.

(C) Positional information for establishing polarity in a human embryo, as in that of the fruit fly, is distributed throughout the egg prior to fertilization.

(D) A study of the development of the fruit fly's visual system would more likely be applicable to questions of human development than would a study of the mechanisms that establish the fruit fly's polarity.

(E) While the fruit fly egg becomes a larva in a single day, a human embryo takes significantly longer to develop because humans cannot develop limbs until they have established a nervous system.

23. According to the passage, polarity is established in a human embryo

(A) after more stages of cell division than in frogs
(B) before the sperm enters the egg
(C) after positional information is provided by the massing of p-granules
(D) by the same sperm-driven mechanism as in the nematode
(E) in the same way as in simpler vertebrates

24. By "conservation of mechanism" (line 48) the author is probably referring to

(A) how the same mechanism can be used to form different parts of the same organism
(B) the fact that no genetic material is wasted in development
(C) how few genes a given organism requires in order to elaborate its parts
(D) a highly complex organism's requiring no more genetic material than a simpler one
(E) the fact that analogous structures in different species are brought about by similar genetic means

25. Which one of the following most accurately states the main purpose of the second paragraph?

(A) to illustrate the diversity of processes by which organisms establish early polarity
(B) to elaborate on the differences between embryonic formation in the fruit fly and in the nematode
(C) to suggest why the process of establishing early polarity in humans is not yet understood
(D) to demonstrate the significance and necessity for genetic development of establishing polarity
(E) to demonstrate that there are two main types of mechanism by which early polarity is established

26. According to the passage, which one of the following is a major difference between the establishment of polarity in the fruit fly and in the nematode?

(A) The fruit fly embryo takes longer to establish polarity than does the nematode embryo.
(B) The mechanisms that establish polarity are more easily identifiable in the nematode than in the fruit fly.
(C) Polarity signals for the fruit fly embryo are inscribed entirely in the egg and these signals for the nematode embryo are inscribed entirely in the sperm.
(D) Polarity in the fruit fly takes more stages of cell division to become established than in the nematode.
(E) Polarity is established for the fruit fly before fertilization and for the nematode through fertilization.

27. The author's primary purpose in the passage is to

(A) articulate a theory of how early polarity is established and support the theory by an analysis of data
(B) describe a phase in the development of organisms in which the genetic mechanisms used are disparate and discuss why this disparity is surprising
(C) provide a classification of the mechanisms by which different life forms establish early polarity
(D) argue that a certain genetic process must occur in all life forms, regardless of their apparent dissimilarity
(E) explain why an embryo must establish early polarity before it can develop into an organism

S T O P

IF YOU FINISH BEFORE TIME IS CALLED, YOU MAY CHECK YOUR WORK ON THIS SECTION ONLY.
DO NOT WORK ON ANY OTHER SECTION IN THE TEST.

SECTION IV

Time—35 minutes

26 Questions

Directions: The questions in this section are based on the reasoning contained in brief statements or passages. For some questions, more than one of the choices could conceivably answer the question. However, you are to choose the best answer; that is, the response that most accurately and completely answers the question. You should not make assumptions that are by commonsense standards implausible, superfluous, or incompatible with the passage. After you have chosen the best answer, blacken the corresponding space on your answer sheet.

1. While 65 percent of the eligible voters who were recently polled favor Perkins over Samuels in the coming election, the results of that poll are dubious because it was not based on a representative sample. Given that Perkins predominantly advocates the interests of the upper-middle class and that the survey was conducted at high-priced shopping malls, it is quite probable that Perkins's supporters were overrepresented.

Which one of the following statements most accurately expresses the main conclusion of the argument?

(A) The poll was intentionally designed to favor Perkins over Samuels.

(B) Samuels's supporters believe that they were probably not adequately represented in the poll.

(C) The poll's results probably do not accurately represent the opinions of the voters in the coming election.

(D) Samuels is quite likely to have a good chance of winning the coming election.

(E) Those who designed the poll should have considered more carefully where to conduct the survey.

2. Sleep research has demonstrated that sleep is characterized by periods of different levels of brain activity. People experience dreams during only one of these periods, known as REM (rapid eye movement) sleep. Test subjects who are chronically deprived of REM sleep become irritable during waking life. This shows that REM sleep relieves the stresses of waking life.

Which one of the following, if true, most strengthens the argument?

(A) Test subjects who are chronically deprived of non-REM sleep also become irritable during waking life.

(B) Chronically having bad dreams can cause stress, but so can chronically having pleasant but exciting dreams.

(C) During times of increased stress, one's REM sleep is disturbed in a way that prevents one from dreaming.

(D) Only some people awakened during REM sleep can report the dreams they were having just before being awakened.

(E) Other factors being equal, people who normally have shorter periods of REM sleep tend to experience more stress.

GO ON TO THE NEXT PAGE.

3. Since 1989 the importation of ivory from African elephants into the United States and Canada has been illegal, but the importation of ivory from the excavated tusks of ancient mammoths remains legal in both countries. Following the ban, there was a sharp increase in the importation of ivory that importers identified as mammoth ivory. In 1989 customs officials lacked a technique for distinguishing elephant ivory from that of mammoths. Just after such a technique was invented and its use by customs officials became widely known, there was a dramatic decrease in the amount of ivory presented for importation into the U.S. and Canada that was identified by importers as mammoth ivory.

Which one of the following is most strongly supported by the information above?

(A) Customs officials still cannot reliably distinguish elephant ivory from mammoth ivory.

(B) Most of the ivory currently imported into the U.S. and Canada comes from neither African elephants nor mammoths.

(C) In the period since the technique for distinguishing elephant ivory from mammoth ivory was implemented, the population of African elephants has declined.

(D) Much of the ivory imported as mammoth ivory just after the ban on ivory from African elephants went into effect was actually elephant ivory.

(E) Shortly after the importation of ivory from African elephants was outlawed, there was a sharp increase in the total amount of all ivory presented for importation into the U.S. and Canada.

4. My suspicion that there is some truth to astrology has been confirmed. Most physicians I have talked to believe in it.

The flawed pattern of reasoning in the argument above is most similar to that in which one of the following?

(A) Professor Smith was convicted of tax evasion last year. So I certainly wouldn't give any credence to Smith's economic theories.

(B) I have come to the conclusion that several governmental social programs are wasteful. This is because most of the biology professors I have discussed this with think that this is true.

(C) Quantum mechanics seems to be emerging as the best physical theory we have today. Most prominent physicists subscribe to it.

(D) Most mechanical engineers I have talked to say that it is healthier to refrain from eating meat. So most mechanical engineers are vegetarians.

(E) For many years now, many people, some famous, have reported that they have seen or come in contact with unidentified flying objects. So there are probably extraterrestrial societies trying to contact us.

5. The best explanation for Mozart's death involves the recently detected fracture in his skull. The crack, most likely the result of an accident, could have easily torn veins in his brain, allowing blood to leak into his brain. When such bleeding occurs in the brain and the blood dries, many of the brain's faculties become damaged, commonly, though not immediately, leading to death. This explanation of Mozart's death is bolstered by the fact that the fracture shows signs of partial healing.

The claim that the fracture shows signs of partial healing figures in the argument in which one of the following ways?

(A) It shows that Mozart's death could have been avoided.

(B) It shows that the fracture did not occur after Mozart's death.

(C) It shows that the dried blood impaired Mozart's brain's faculties.

(D) It shows that Mozart's death occurred suddenly.

(E) It suggests that Mozart's death was accidental.

6. In the first phase of the Industrial Revolution, machines were invented whose main advantage was that they worked faster than human workers. This technology became widely used because it was economically attractive; many unskilled workers could be replaced by just a few skilled workers. Today managers are looking for technology that will allow them to replace highly paid skilled workers with a smaller number of less-skilled workers.

The examples presented above best illustrate which one of the following propositions?

(A) Employers utilize new technology because it allows them to reduce labor costs.

(B) Workers will need to acquire more education and skills to remain competitive in the labor market.

(C) In seeking employment, highly skilled workers no longer have an advantage over less-skilled workers.

(D) Technology eliminates many jobs but also creates just as many jobs.

(E) Whereas technological innovations were once concentrated in heavy industry, they now affect all industries.

GO ON TO THE NEXT PAGE.

7. For many types of crops, hybrid strains have been developed that have been found in test plantings to produce significantly higher yields than were produced by traditional nonhybrid strains of those crops planted alongside them. However, in many parts of the world where farmers have abandoned traditional nonhybrid strains in favor of the hybrid strains, crop yields have not increased.

Which one of the following, if true, most helps to resolve the apparent discrepancy?

(A) Most farmers who plant the hybrid strains of their crops have larger farms than do farmers who continue to plant traditional nonhybrid strains of the same crops.

(B) Hybrid strains of crops produced higher yields in some areas than did nonhybrid strains in those areas.

(C) The hybrid strains were tested under significantly better farming conditions than are found in most areas where farmers grow those strains.

(D) Many traditional nonhybrid strains of plants produce crops that taste better and thus sell better than the hybrid strains of those crops.

(E) Many governments subsidize farmers who plant only hybrid strains of staple crops.

8. This stamp is probably highly valuable, since it exhibits a printing error. The most important factors in determining a stamp's value, assuming it is in good condition, are its rarity and age. This is clearly a fine specimen, and it is quite old as well.

The conclusion is properly inferred if which one of the following is assumed?

(A) The older a stamp is, the more valuable it is.
(B) Printing errors are always confined to a few individual stamps.
(C) Most stamps with printing errors are already in the hands of collectors.
(D) Rarity and age are of equal importance to a stamp's value.
(E) Even old and rare stamps are usually not valuable if they are in poor condition.

9. A recent study of several hundred female physicians showed that their tendency to develop coronary disease was inversely proportional to their dietary intake of two vitamins, folate and B6. The researchers concluded that folate and B6 inhibit the development of heart disease in women.

Which one of the following would, if true, most weaken the researchers' conclusion?

(A) The foods that contain significant amounts of the vitamins folate and B6 also contain significant amounts of nonvitamin nutrients that inhibit heart disease.

(B) It is very unlikely that a chemical compound would inhibit coronary disease in women but not in men.

(C) Physicians are more likely than nonphysicians to know a great deal about the link between diet and health.

(D) The physicians in the study had not been screened in advance to ensure that none had preexisting heart conditions.

(E) The vitamins folate and B6 are present only in very small amounts in most foods.

10. The proposed coal-burning electric plant should be approved, since no good arguments have been offered against it. After all, all the arguments against it have been presented by competing electricity producers.

Which one of the following is an assumption on which the reasoning above depends?

(A) The competing electricity producers would stand to lose large amounts of revenue from the building of the coal-burning electric plant.

(B) If a person's arguments against a proposal are defective, then that person has a vested interest in seeing that the proposal is not implemented.

(C) Approval of the coal-burning electric plant would please coal suppliers more than disapproval would please suppliers of fuel to the competing electricity producers.

(D) If good arguments are presented for a proposal, then that proposal should be approved.

(E) Arguments made by those who have a vested interest in the outcome of a proposal are not good arguments.

GO ON TO THE NEXT PAGE.

11. Psychiatrist: While the first appearance of a phobia is usually preceded by a traumatizing event, not everyone who is traumatized by an event develops a phobia. Furthermore, many people with phobias have never been traumatized. These two considerations show that traumatizing events do not contribute to the occurrence of phobias.

The reasoning in the psychiatrist's argument is most vulnerable to criticism on the grounds that the argument

(A) treats the cause of the occurrence of a type of phenomenon as an effect of phenomena of that type

(B) presumes, without providing justification, that some psychological events have no causes that can be established by scientific investigation

(C) builds the conclusion drawn into the support cited for that conclusion

(D) takes for granted that a type of phenomenon contributes to the occurrence of another type of phenomenon only if phenomena of these two types are invariably associated

(E) derives a causal connection from mere association when there is no independent evidence of causal connection

12. Some species are called "indicator species" because the loss of a population of such a species serves as an early warning of problems arising from pollution. Environmentalists tracking the effects of pollution have increasingly paid heed to indicator species; yet environmentalists would be misguided if they attributed the loss of a population to pollution in all cases. Though declines in population often do signal environmental degradation, they are just as often a result of the natural evolution of an ecosystem. We must remember that, in nature, change is the status quo.

Which one of the following most accurately expresses the argument's conclusion?

(A) Environmentalists sometimes overreact to the loss of a specific population.

(B) The loss of a specific population should not always be interpreted as a sign of environmental degradation.

(C) Environmentalists' use of indicator species in tracking the effects of pollution is often problematic.

(D) The loss of a specific population is often the result of natural changes in an ecosystem and in such cases should not be resisted.

(E) The loss of a specific population as a result of pollution is simply part of nature's status quo.

13. Columnist: Tagowa's testimony in the Pemberton trial was not heard outside the courtroom, so we cannot be sure what she said. Afterward, however, she publicly affirmed her belief in Pemberton's guilt. Hence, since the jury found Pemberton not guilty, we can conclude that not all of the jury members believed Tagowa's testimony.

Which one of the following describes a flaw in the columnist's reasoning?

(A) It overlooks that a witness may think that a defendant is guilty even though that witness's testimony in no way implicates the defendant.

(B) It confuses facts about what certain people believe with facts about what ought to be the case.

(C) It presumes, without providing warrant, that juries find defendants guilty only if those defendants committed the crimes with which they are charged.

(D) It presumes, without providing warrant, that a jury's finding a defendant not guilty is evidence of dishonesty on the part of someone who testified against the defendant.

(E) It fails to consider that jury members sometimes disagree with each other about the significance of a particular person's testimony.

14. A new tax law aimed at encouraging the reforestation of cleared land in order to increase the amount of forested land in a particular region offers lumber companies tax incentives for each unit of cleared land they reforest. One lumber company has accordingly reduced its tax liability by purchasing a large tract of cleared land in the region and reforesting it. The company paid for the purchase by clearing a larger tract of land in the region, a tract that it had planned to hold in long-term reserve.

If the statements above are true, which one of the following must be true about the new tax law?

(A) It is a failure in encouraging the reforestation of cleared land in the region.

(B) It will have no immediate effect on the amount of forested land in the region.

(C) It will ultimately cause lumber companies to plant trees on approximately as much land as they harvest in the region.

(D) It can provide a motivation for companies to act in a manner contrary to the purpose of the law while taking advantage of the tax incentives.

(E) It will provide lumber companies with a tax incentive that will ultimately be responsible for a massive decrease in the number of mature forests in the region.

GO ON TO THE NEXT PAGE.

15. Trustee: The recent exhibit at the art museum was extensively covered by the local media, and this coverage seems to have contributed to the record-breaking attendance it drew. If the attendance at the exhibit had been low, the museum would have gone bankrupt and closed permanently, so the museum could not have remained open had it not been for the coverage from the local media.

The reasoning in the trustee's argument is most vulnerable to criticism on the grounds that the argument

(A) confuses a necessary condition for the museum's remaining open with a sufficient condition for the museum's remaining open

(B) takes for granted that no previous exhibit at the museum had received such extensive media coverage

(C) takes for granted that most people who read articles about the exhibit also attended the exhibit

(D) fails to address the possibility that the exhibit would have drawn enough visitors to prevent bankruptcy even without media coverage

(E) presupposes the very conclusion that it is trying to prove

16. Economist: A tax is effective if it raises revenue and burdens all and only those persons targeted by the tax. A tax is ineffective, however, if it does not raise revenue and it costs a significant amount of money to enforce.

Which one of the following inferences is most strongly supported by the principles stated by the economist?

(A) The tax on cigarettes burdens most, but not all, of the people targeted by it. Thus, if it raises revenue, the tax is effective.

(B) The tax on alcohol raises a modest amount of revenue, but it costs a significant amount of money to enforce. Thus, the tax is ineffective.

(C) The tax on gasoline costs a significant amount of money to enforce. Thus, if it does not raise revenue, the tax is ineffective.

(D) The tax on coal burdens all of the people targeted by it, and this tax does not burden anyone who is not targeted by it. Thus, the tax is effective.

(E) The tax on steel does not cost a significant amount of money to enforce, but it does not raise revenue either. Thus, the tax is ineffective.

17. A large amount of rainfall in April and May typically leads to an increase in the mosquito population and thus to an increased threat of encephalitis. People cannot change the weather. Thus people cannot decrease the threat of encephalitis.

The reasoning in the argument above is flawed in that the argument

(A) takes for granted that because one event precedes another the former must be the cause of the latter

(B) presumes, without providing justification, that a certain outcome would be desirable

(C) ignores the possibility that a certain type of outcome is dependent on more than one factor

(D) takes for granted that a threat that is aggravated by certain factors could not occur in the absence of those factors

(E) draws a conclusion about what is possible from a premise about what is actually the case

18. Leadership depends as much on making one's followers aware of their own importance as it does on conveying a vivid image of a collective goal. Only if they are convinced both that their efforts are necessary for the accomplishment of this goal, and that these efforts, if expended, will actually achieve it, will people follow a leader.

If all of the statements above are true, then which one of the following CANNOT be true?

(A) Some leaders who convince their followers of the necessity of their efforts in achieving a goal fail, nevertheless, to lead them to the attainment of that goal.

(B) One who succeeds in conveying to one's followers the relationship between their efforts and the attainment of a collective goal succeeds in leading these people to this goal.

(C) Only if one is a leader must one convince people of the necessity of their efforts for the attainment of a collective goal.

(D) Sometimes people succeed in achieving a collective goal without ever having been convinced that by trying to do so they would succeed.

(E) Sometimes people who remain unsure of whether their efforts are needed for the attainment of a collective goal nevertheless follow a leader.

GO ON TO THE NEXT PAGE.

19. Fifty chronic insomniacs participated in a one-month study conducted at an institute for sleep disorders. Half were given a dose of a new drug and the other half were given a placebo every night before going to bed at the institute. Approximately 80 percent of the participants in each group reported significant relief from insomnia during the first two weeks of the study. But in each group, approximately 90 percent of those who had reported relief claimed that their insomnia had returned during the third week of the study.

Which one of the following, if true, most helps to explain all the data from the study?

(A) Because it is easy to build up a tolerance to the new drug, most people will no longer experience its effects after taking it every night for two weeks.

(B) The psychological comfort afforded by the belief that one has taken a sleep-promoting drug is enough to prevent most episodes of insomnia.

(C) The new drug is very similar in chemical composition to another drug, large doses of which have turned out to be less effective than expected.

(D) Most insomniacs sleep better in a new environment, and the new drug has no effect on an insomniac's ability to sleep.

(E) Some insomniacs cannot reliably determine how much sleep they have had or how well they have slept.

20. Advertisement: The Country Classic is the only kind of car in its class that offers an antilock braking system that includes TrackAid. An antilock braking system keeps your wheels from locking up during hard braking, and TrackAid keeps your rear wheels from spinning on slippery surfaces. So if you are a safety-conscious person in the market for a car in this class, the Country Classic is the only car for you.

The advertisement is misleading if which one of the following is true?

(A) All of the cars that are in the same class as the Country Classic offer some kind of antilock braking system.

(B) Most kinds of cars that are in the same class as the Country Classic are manufactured by the same company that manufactures the Country Classic.

(C) Without an antilock braking system, the wheels of the Country Classic and other cars in its class are more likely to lock up during hard braking than they are to spin on slippery surfaces.

(D) Other cars in the same class as the Country Classic offer an antilock braking system that uses a method other than TrackAid to prevent rear wheels from spinning on slippery surfaces.

(E) The Country Classic is more expensive than any other car in its class.

21. Sociologist: Traditional norms in our society prevent sincerity by requiring one to ignore unpleasant realities and tell small lies. But a community whose members do not trust one another cannot succeed. So, if a community is to succeed, its members must be willing to face unpleasant realities and speak about them honestly.

The sociologist's conclusion follows logically if which one of the following is assumed?

(A) Sincerity is required if community members are to trust each other.

(B) The more sincere and open community members are, the more likely that community is to succeed.

(C) A community sometimes can succeed even if its members subscribe to traditional norms.

(D) Unless a community's members are willing to face unpleasant realities, they cannot be sincere.

(E) A community's failure is often caused by its members' unwillingness to face unpleasant realities and to discuss them honestly.

GO ON TO THE NEXT PAGE.

22. If there is an election, you can either vote or not. If you vote, you have the satisfaction of knowing you influenced the results of the election; if you do not vote, you have no right to complain about the results. So, following an election, either you will have the satisfaction of knowing you influenced its results or you will have no right to complain.

The reasoning in which one of the following most closely resembles that in the argument above?

(A) When you rent a car, you can either take out insurance or not. If you take out insurance you are covered, but if you are uninsured, you are personally liable for any costs incurred from an accident. So in case of an accident, you will be better off if you are insured.

(B) If you go for a walk, when you are finished either you will feel relaxed or you will not. If you feel relaxed, then your muscles will likely not be sore the next day, though your muscles will more likely become conditioned faster if they do feel sore. Therefore, either your muscles will feel sore, or they will become better conditioned.

(C) If you attend school, you will find the courses stimulating or you will not. If your teachers are motivated, you will find the courses stimulating. If your teachers are not motivated, you will not. So either your teachers are motivated, or their courses are not stimulating.

(D) If you use a computer, its messages are either easily readable or not. If the messages are easily readable, they are merely password protected. If they are not easily readable, they are electronically encrypted. So any message on the computer you use is either password protected or electronically encrypted.

(E) When manufacturers use a natural resource, they are either efficient or inefficient. If they are inefficient, the resource will be depleted quickly. If they are efficient, the resource will last much longer. So either manufacturers are efficient or they should be fined.

23. Company president: Our consultants report that, in general, the most efficient managers have excellent time management skills. Thus, to improve productivity I recommend that we make available to our middle-level managers a seminar to train them in techniques of time management.

Each of the following, if true, would weaken the support for the company president's recommendation EXCEPT:

(A) The consultants use the same criteria to evaluate managers' efficiency as they do to evaluate their time management skills.

(B) Successful time management is more dependent on motivation than on good technique.

(C) Most managers at other companies who have attended time management seminars are still unproductive.

(D) Most managers who are already efficient do not need to improve their productivity.

(E) Most managers who are efficient have never attended a time management seminar.

24. Many Seychelles warblers of breeding age forgo breeding, remaining instead with their parents and helping to raise their own siblings. This behavior, called cooperative breeding, results from the scarcity of nesting territory for the birds on the tiny island that, until recently, was home to the world's population of Seychelles warblers. Yet when healthy warblers were transplanted to a much larger neighboring island as part of an experiment, most of those warblers maintained a pattern of cooperative breeding.

Which one of the following, if true, most helps to explain the result of the experiment?

(A) Many of the Seychelles warblers that were transplanted to the neighboring island had not yet reached breeding age.

(B) The climate of the island to which Seychelles warblers were transplanted was the same as that of the warblers' native island.

(C) Most of the terrain on the neighboring island was not of the type in which Seychelles warblers generally build their nests.

(D) Cooperative breeding in species other than the Seychelles warbler often results when the environment cannot sustain a rise in the population.

(E) The Seychelles warblers had fewer competitors for nesting territory on the island to which they were transplanted than on their native island.

GO ON TO THE NEXT PAGE.

25. Therapist: In a recent study, researchers measured how quickly 60 different psychological problems waned as a large, diverse sample of people underwent weekly behavioral therapy sessions. About 75 percent of the 60 problems consistently cleared up within 50 weeks of therapy. This shows that 50 weekly behavioral therapy sessions are all that most people need.

The therapist's argument is logically most vulnerable to criticism on the grounds that it

(A) takes for granted that there are no psychological problems that usually take significantly longer to clear up than the 60 psychological problems studied

(B) fails to address the possibility that any given one of the 60 psychological problems studied might afflict most people

(C) takes for granted that no one suffers from more than one of the 60 psychological problems studied

(D) fails to address the possibility that some forms of therapy have never been proven to be effective as treatments for psychological problems

(E) takes for granted that the sample of people studied did not have significantly more psychological problems, on average, than the population as a whole

26. Researcher: It is commonly believed that species belonging to the same biological order, such as rodents, descended from a single common ancestor. However, I compared the genetic pattern in 3 rodent species—guinea pigs, rats, and mice—as well as in 13 nonrodent mammals, and found that while rats and mice are genetically quite similar, the genetic differences between guinea pigs and mice are as great as those between mice and some nonrodent species. Thus, despite their similar physical form, guinea pigs stem from a separate ancestor.

Which one of the following, if true, most seriously undermines the researcher's reasoning?

(A) The researcher examined the genetic material of only 3 of over 2,000 species of rodents.

(B) Some pairs of species not having a common ancestor are genetically more similar to each other than are some pairs that do have a common ancestor.

(C) The researcher selected nonrodent species that have the specific cell structures she wanted to analyze genetically, though many nonrodent mammals lack these cell structures.

(D) For some genuine biological orders, the most recent common ancestor dates from later epochs than does the most recent common ancestor of other biological orders.

(E) Peculiarities of body structure, such as distinctive teeth and olfactory structures, are shared by all rodents, including guinea pigs.

S T O P

IF YOU FINISH BEFORE TIME IS CALLED, YOU MAY CHECK YOUR WORK ON THIS SECTION ONLY.
DO NOT WORK ON ANY OTHER SECTION IN THE TEST.

Acknowledgment is made to the following sources from which material has been adapted for use in this test booklet:

Natalie Angier, "Heads or Tails? How Embryos Get It Right." ©1995 by The New York Times.

Catherine Bell, "Aboriginal Claims to Cultural Property in Canada: A Comparative Legal Analysis of the Repatriation Debate." ©1992 by the American Indian Law Review.

Louise Glück, *Proofs & Theories: Essays on Poetry*. ©1994 by Louise Glück.

"Why Bad Hair Days May Not Matter." ©1996 by Sussex Publishers Inc.

Wait for the supervisor's instructions before you open the page to the topic.
Please print and sign your name and write the date in the designated spaces below.

Time: 35 Minutes

General Directions

You will have 35 minutes in which to plan and write an essay on the topic inside. Read the topic and the accompanying directions carefully. You will probably find it best to spend a few minutes considering the topic and organizing your thoughts before you begin writing. In your essay, be sure to develop your ideas fully, leaving time, if possible, to review what you have written. **Do not write on a topic other than the one specified. Writing on a topic of your own choice is not acceptable.**

No special knowledge is required or expected for this writing exercise. Law schools are interested in the reasoning, clarity, organization, language usage, and writing mechanics displayed in your essay. How well you write is more important than how much you write.

Confine your essay to the blocked, lined area on the front and back of the separate writing sample response sheet. Only that area will be reproduced for law schools. Be sure that your writing is legible.

Both this topic sheet and your response sheet must be turned over to the testing staff before you leave the room.

LSAC®

Topic Code	Print Your Full Name Here		
011338	Last	First	M.I.

Date	Sign Your Name Here
/ /	

Scratch Paper
Do not write your essay in this space.

LSAT® WRITING SAMPLE TOPICS

Each candidate who took the December 2005 LSAT received *one* of the two writing sample topics below. These topics include one example of each of two different kinds of writing prompt—decision or argument. The two topics were randomly distributed among all test takers at the December 2005 LSAT administration as part of LSAC's ongoing research and development of effective writing sample prompts. Prompts of these kinds may or may not appear on future LSATs. Advance notice of the kinds of prompts that may appear at each LSAT administration can be found at *www.LSAC.org*.

Directions: The scenario presented below describes two choices, either one of which can be supported on the basis of the information given. Your essay should consider both choices and argue <u>for</u> one and <u>against</u> the other, based on the two specified criteria and the facts provided. There is no "right" or "wrong" choice: a reasonable argument can be made for either.

The owner of Avanti Pizza, which currently makes pizzas for pickup or delivery only, is considering expanding his business. He can either purchase a brick pizza oven or he can add a small dining room to his restaurant. Write an essay in which you argue for one option over the other, keeping in mind the following two criteria:

- Avanti's owner wants to increase profits by offering customers something of value that Avanti does not currently provide.
- Avanti's owner wants to distinguish his restaurant from local competitors.

Brick-oven pizza has become extremely popular, and Avanti's owner estimates that including it on the menu would substantially increase takeout and delivery business. The profit margin on such pizzas is higher than that on conventional pizzas. In addition, Avanti's pizza chef could use the opportunity to introduce a selection of gourmet pizzas with creative toppings. Avanti's competitors consist of a well-established Italian restaurant, La Stella, and a franchisee of the large pizza delivery chain Pronto. Neither has a brick oven, although La Stella is rumored to be considering the option. The new oven could be up and running two weeks after the start of construction.

Avanti does not currently have space for a dining room, but the adjacent storefront property has recently become available on good lease terms. Obtaining permits and remodeling would take six months to a year, during which time the rest of the business could continue to operate. Avanti's chef would like to expand the menu to include dishes other than pizza, and with an eat-in option for customers she could easily do so. La Stella already offers sit-down dining, but in a relatively formal setting. Avanti could be more relaxed and family-friendly. In addition, Avanti could allow patrons to bring their own wine or beer, which would attract economy-minded customers. La Stella, which has a liquor license and a full bar, charges a substantial markup on all the alcoholic beverages it serves.

Directions: For this essay you are presented with an argument that offers reasons for drawing a particular conclusion. Your essay should analyze and evaluate the line of reasoning and use of evidence in the argument. For example, you may want to discuss how the logic of the argument is flawed or could be improved, or what counterexamples or alternative explanations would undermine the argument. You may also want to consider what, if any, questionable assumptions underlie the reasoning and what additional information or evidence may have been overlooked that would strengthen or weaken the argument. *Note that you are not being asked to present your personal opinion on the subject with which the argument is concerned.*

Editorial:

"The number of indictments of top business executives for corporate misdeeds has been higher in the last several years than at any previous time in recent history. Much of the blame for this sorry state of affairs must be laid at the doorstep of business schools. It can hardly be a coincidence that the number of executives holding MBA (Master of Business Administration) degrees is higher than ever before. At the same time, the curricula of business schools have increasingly come to be dominated by courses in economics. The problem is that economics is as neutral with regard to issues of morality as is physics or chemistry. The only way to combat the decline in corporate morality is to require business schools to teach more courses in ethics."

Discuss how well reasoned you find this argument.

Directions:

1. Use the Answer Key on the next page to check your answers.

2. Use the Scoring Worksheet below to compute your raw score.

3. Use the Score Conversion Chart to convert your raw score into the 120-180 scale.

Scoring Worksheet

1. Enter the number of questions you answered correctly in each section.

	Number Correct
SECTION I	_____
SECTION II	_____
SECTION III	_____
SECTION IV	_____

2. Enter the sum here: _____

   This is your Raw Score.

Conversion Chart
For Converting Raw Score to the 120-180 LSAT Scaled Score
LSAT Form 5LSN66

Reported Score	Raw Score Lowest	Raw Score Highest
180	100	101
179	—*	—*
178	99	99
177	98	98
176	—*	—*
175	97	97
174	96	96
173	—*	—*
172	95	95
171	94	94
170	93	93
169	92	92
168	90	91
167	89	89
166	88	88
165	86	87
164	85	85
163	83	84
162	81	82
161	80	80
160	78	79
159	76	77
158	74	75
157	72	73
156	70	71
155	68	69
154	66	67
153	64	65
152	62	63
151	60	61
150	58	59
149	56	57
148	54	55
147	52	53
146	50	51
145	49	49
144	47	48
143	45	46
142	43	44
141	41	42
140	39	40
139	38	38
138	36	37
137	34	35
136	33	33
135	31	32
134	30	30
133	29	29
132	27	28
131	26	26
130	25	25
129	23	24
128	22	22
127	21	21
126	20	20
125	19	19
124	18	18
123	17	17
122	16	16
121	15	15
120	0	14

*There is no raw score that will produce this scaled score for this form.

SECTION I

1.	D	8.	C	15.	A	22.	E
2.	D	9.	D	16.	D	23.	E
3.	C	10.	D	17.	E	24.	E
4.	B	11.	E	18.	D	25.	C
5.	A	12.	B	19.	B	26.	A
6.	A	13.	C	20.	E		
7.	C	14.	D	21.	B		

SECTION II

1.	C	8.	B	15.	D	22.	B
2.	E	9.	C	16.	C		
3.	E	10.	E	17.	C		
4.	A	11.	D	18.	A		
5.	A	12.	E	19.	A		
6.	A	13.	C	20.	A		
7.	C	14.	A	21.	D		

SECTION III

1.	A	8.	C	15.	E	22.	D
2.	D	9.	A	16.	D	23.	A
3.	E	10.	C	17.	D	24.	E
4.	B	11.	E	18.	A	25.	A
5.	C	12.	D	19.	C	26.	E
6.	D	13.	B	20.	C	27.	B
7.	E	14.	C	21.	C		

SECTION IV

1.	C	8.	B	15.	D	22.	D
2.	E	9.	A	16.	C	23.	D
3.	D	10.	E	17.	C	24.	C
4.	B	11.	D	18.	E	25.	B
5.	B	12.	B	19.	D	26.	B
6.	A	13.	A	20.	D		
7.	C	14.	D	21.	A		

LSAT® Prep Tools

LSAT **ItemWise®**

Get to know the LSAT

LSAC's popular, online LSAT familiarization tool, *LSAT ItemWise*:

- includes all three types of LSAT questions—logical reasoning, analytical reasoning, and reading comprehension;

- keeps track of your answers; and

- shows you explanations as to why answers are correct or incorrect.

Although it is best to use our paper-and-pencil *Official LSAT PrepTest®* products to fully prepare for the LSAT, you can enhance your preparation by understanding all three question types and why your answers are right or wrong.

ItemWise includes an introduction to the new reading comprehension question type—comparative reading—with sample questions and explanations.

LSAC account holders get unlimited online access to *ItemWise* for the length of the account.

$18 (at *www.LSAC.org*)